FEARLESS pregnancy

FEARLESS pregnancy

Wisdom and Reassurance from a Doctor, a Midwife, and a Mom

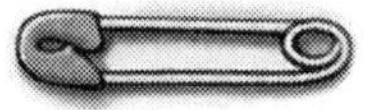

Victoria Clayton, Stuart Fischbein, M.D., F.A.C.O.G.,
Joyce Weckl, M.S.N., C.N.M.

FAIR WINDS
PRESS
GLOUCESTER, MASSACHUSETTS

First published in the USA in 2004 by
Fair Winds Press
33 Commercial Street
Gloucester, MA 01930

08 07 06 05 04 1 2 3 4 5

ISBN 1-59233-079-7

Library of Congress Cataloging-in-Publication Data

Clayton, Victoria.
Fearless pregnancy : wisdom and reassurance from a doctor, a midwife, and a mom / Victoria Clayton, Stuart Fischbein, Joyce Weckl.
p. cm.
ISBN 1-59233-079-7
1. Pregnancy--Popular works. 2. Pregnant women--Health and hygiene--Popular works. I. Fischbein, Stuart. II. Weckl, Joyce. III. Title.
RG525.C644 2004
618.2--dc22
2004020651

Illustrations by Melissa Placzek
Book design by Laura H. Couallier, Laura Herrmann Design

Printed and bound in Canada

The information in this book is for educational purposes only.
It is not intended to replace the advice of a physician or medical practitioner.

FOR

Nicolas Emerson Alexander
Born August 18, 2003

Madeleine Anna Fischbein
Born November 30, 1996

Claire Elyse Weckl
Born June 7, 1997

And your baby

Contents

ACKNOWLEDGMENTS *viii*

CHAPTER 1: The Pregnancy Fear Factor *11*

CHAPTER 2: A Fearless Beginning *21*

CHAPTER 3: Fearless Prenatal Testing *45*

CHAPTER 4: Fearless Diet, Weight Gain, and Exercise *75*

CHAPTER 5: Fearless Maternity Fashion *107*

CHAPTER 6: Fearless (Pregnant) Living *119*

CHAPTER 7: Fearless Gear Buying *153*

CHAPTER 8: Fearless Delivery Prep *177*

CHAPTER 9: Nine Common Problems—
And Why You Shouldn't Fear Them *211*

CHAPTER 10: Fearless Techniques for Relieving Stress *219*

CHAPTER 11: Fearless Postpartum (Epilogue) *231*

INDEX *247*

RESOURCES *255*

ABOUT THE AUTHORS *256*

Acknowledgments

Thank you to my husband Michael Alexander for his love and unwavering confidence. Of course, thank you dear Nicolas for being my inspiration and teacher. And for their TLC with Nicolas (and Celia), much gratitude to Nana Lori, Papa Bill, Juli, Paul, and Melanie Raabe. Thank you to all the Chicks Who Click/Moms Who Click for their encouragement. Without the medical expertise, sanity and compassion of co-authors Stuart Fischbein and Joyce Weckl, as well as the editing skills of Donna Raskin and Holly Schmidt, there wouldn't be *Fearless Pregnancy.* You're all dreams to work with. Lastly, thank you to my mother and all women who have had the courage to take this journey.

– Victoria Clayton

For their honesty, wisdom and extremely valuable time, the fearless moms who contributed their anecdotes and questions to this book deserve more than a thank you. But since that's all we have, THANK YOU to: Amy Hayashi-Jones, Andie Kallinger, Angela Lang, Anne Scheck, Donna Raskin, Dorothy Peters, Hadley Fierlinger, Jacqueline Stenson, Jane Goodstein, Jane Tucker, Jenna Coito, Jennifer McClure-Metz, Jennifer Schonbrunn Hinkle, Jodi Osburn, Jodi Torres, JoAnna Johnson, Karen Kin Hartstein, Kathryn Alice, Kim Martin, Laura Ludwig, Lisa Loop, Livia Hanich, Renee Mancino, Sarah Metz, Sorrel Sammons and Vicki Alderete.

From the Fearless Doc

To my parents, my sister Susan, and my family and friends back home in Minnesota who taught me the virtues of common sense. To David Kline, M.D., Kristine Kelly, and Maureen Faulkner for their knowledge and support. To Max, Alex, Andy, and Madeleine for providing my inspiration. Finally, to Victoria and Joyce for their devotion to the betterment of women's health.

– Stuart Fischbein, M.D., F.A.C.O.G.

From the Fearless Midwife

Thank you to my family, but especially to my mom and my daughter, the two females in this world who have taught me the importance of love, acceptance, and good mothering. To all of the women I've worked with, for the honor of being a part of their lives. To Victoria, for making all of this possible, and to Stuart, for making my dream of midwifery and loving care for women a reality.

– Joyce Weckl, M.S.N., C.N.M.

1

The Pregnancy Fear Factor

"What are fears but voices airy?
Whispering harm where harm is not."

—Wordsworth

Imagine an apparently healthy, pregnant woman strolling down the street. You see her hand gently resting on her belly as she stops to gaze in a store window. Take a guess at what she's thinking. It'd be sane to assume that she's happily dreaming of the arrival of her child, planning the nursery perhaps. In fact, it's more likely that only half of the time is she thinking something close to this. Since you're pregnant, you probably already realize that the other half of the time this pregnant woman is worrying!

Worry is a byproduct of fear. And in the age of so much information (and misinformation), pregnant women can hardly help but be fearful. You're being bombarded with precautionary advice, admonishments, and warnings, most of which are unnecessary. Here, then, is something very important to understand about fear: it's normal (to a certain extent), but not something you have to buy into.

Of course, absolutely everybody worries. Fear has an evolutionary purpose, in fact. It prioritizes your life and ensures that you pay close attention to the right things. It even blends with your intuition to motivate you to act or not act in certain situations. So in pregnancy, as in life, some fear makes you take better care of yourself and your developing baby.

The key is that the *fear must be valid, and it must be used properly—to inquire, explore, and act wisely.* A very real problem in pregnancy these days is that much of the fear you experience is, as Wordsworth said, just an airy (and

What's the Fearless Pregnancy *Payoff?*

The payoff to quashing your pregnancy fears is, of course, that you'll have a less stressed and more vibrant pregnancy. But that's not all. When you make a decision to stand and face pregnancy fears—name the real ones, act on them, and then discredit the false ones—you're contributing to the potential for all women to experience more joyful pregnancies. You're helping to remove the veil of mystery and negativity that shrouds pregnancy and childbirth.

annoying, we might add) voice. It's not a healthful variety of fear—or about anything that you can actually act on. Instead, it's based on false premises and does nothing to motivate you to live better. It only causes undo stress and angst. Where does this unnecessary fear come from?

A Mommy Perk: Maternal-Induced Neural Plasticity

That's researcher-speak for "pregnancy will make you more ingenious and courageous." A study recently published in the journal *Physiology and Behavior* found that female rats that have had one or more litters are much less stressed when provoked than rats without pups. When the neuro-scientist examined the rats, he found much less activity in the fear centers of mother rats' brains. They were calmer and braver, according to the researcher. Furthermore, previous studies have shown that pregnancy hormones seem to nurture brain cells involved in learning and memory. Mother rats did better than their virgin sisters in a rat maze test. So get ready for a little maternal-induced neural plasticity!

The Origins of Pregnancy Fear

Fear comes from two distinct places: your internal world of anxiety and worry and the external world imposed on you. Internally, we all have worries about our abilities in this world and our abilities as pregnant women. Even the lionesses among us may be overwhelmed by fear when they see that little line on the home pregnancy test and realize, yes, indeed, they will soon be somebody's mom. There's the moment of pink-line exhilaration (yes, we did it!), but when that wanes, in comes the deafening internal scream that says, "Oh my God, what have we done?"

This reaction is simply human nature, especially when you're embarking on a new journey that is probably the most important journey of your life. In fact, it's our desires that often give birth, so to speak, to many of our worries.

From about the time of your first menstrual period, the female body desires to conceive. From a purely biological standpoint, if you're pregnant right now, you're fulfilling your only purpose on the planet: to reproduce. Many women are deciding not to have children, of course, but for most of us being a mother is still a heartfelt desire. The greater the yearning is, the more intense the fear sometimes feels. This is the root of much of the internal fear—pregnancy is something you desperately want but just can't control.

Your Baby Has Already Won

Pregnancy was not always filled with cautionary advice. As recently as the 1960s, women smoked and drank alcohol throughout pregnancy. They ate whatever they wanted, worked in dangerous conditions, didn't know much about the process of childbirth, and yet managed to have healthy children. Historically, women rode cross-country in covered wagons, braved the elements, and delivered their babies in remote wilderness areas. Even today women live in war-torn countries, suffer from starvation and deadly illnesses, have serious drug addictions, and still manage to give birth most often to healthy babies. So the clear fact is that babies of mothers like you—women who are taking care of themselves, avoiding intoxicants, getting prenatal care, eating well, and living in ideal conditions—have won the lottery. Congratulations!

Today, we have the best medical care and living conditions ever. Clearly, your chances of having a normal, healthy baby are as good as they've ever been. Yet somewhere along the line, most popular books and magazines, even family and friends, don't seem to recognize this. Your sisters relay horrific labor stories; your mother voices concern over your eating habits; friends at the gym warn you not to do this and that—it seems everyone wants to help you, and in the process they scare you to death! Even well-meaning strangers will enthrall you with odd stories of other pregnant women or some study they've heard about. Most of this, believe it or not, comes from concern and love.

Often people's own fears and insecurities compel them to relay these tales. The reason any of these stories are noteworthy, however, is that they have a bizarre twist or are at least out of the ordinary. They are also most often medically inaccurate. Many people get their facts wrong or misperceive a situation. Like the game of telephone, where the message gets more convoluted as it gets passed along, so too do pregnancy and birth horror stories. The truth is, most obstetrical emergencies are as rare as or even rarer than being struck by lightning. Try as you might, though, it's tough to prevent this negativity from affecting you.

Even the medical world plays its part in instilling fear in pregnant women. Incredible technology—from prenatal tests to sonograms to devices used during delivery—has the ultimate goal of providing you with the safest and best care. Great comfort can, in fact, be found in these tests and equipment—if they provide you with good news, that is. But what happens when they come back with uncertain conclusions or you don't fully understand the results? Suddenly the very technology that is supposed to make you feel safer scares you. For example, fetal monitoring was introduced to provide better outcomes for babies during labor. Often women and their partners will have their eyes fixed on the monitor, fearing any irregular beat. Most irregularities on a fetal monitor mean nothing, but to the untrained eye or ear they incite needless panic.

Another major contributor to the anxieties pregnant women feel comes from a piece of paper handed to you by your doctor. It's called an "informed consent" form. Simply put, because of the fear of medical malpractice lawsuits, we now have a document that outlines all of the possible things that have ever been known to happen after a test, procedure, or treatment. Sometimes, even events that have never really happened but could possibly happen must be discussed. So we now have long-winded documents that can't possibly be completely understood but that sow ideas of absurdly remote risks.

And, believe it or not, some aspects of pregnancy education can also be blamed for fueling fear. Sometimes, in books meant to educate and even in classes geared to pregnant women, fear-based advice is doled out: Don't pump your own gas. Don't eat sushi. Don't color your hair. Don't exercise. Don't pet your cat. Too often these sources are filled with warnings from well-meaning people who simply aren't qualified to give them.

What does all this fear do to you?

We've Come a Long Way, Baby

Despite the abundance of poorly interpreted information, misinformation, and fear-generating half-truths, we must also appreciate the progress we've made during the last thirty or so years. Much of this is due to the feminist movement in the 1970s. With feminism came the first childbirth education classes. Most of the early classes were developed by advocates for non-medicated births. The line of thinking was that knowledge would give women power and reduce fear, which would allow them to deliver their babies more easily. These classes have helped countless couples appreciate and experience the birthing process in a far healthier way. (Sometimes they've had the opposite effect too, but we'll get to that later.) We owe these early trailblazers enormous gratitude. They're the reason you're not covered in a tent dress and are, instead, celebrating your pregnant body, experiences, and challenges.

The Number One Fear-Fighting Weapon:

Confidence in Your Doctor/Midwife

The best way to counteract fear is to receive health care from someone you trust in the setting that makes you comfortable. Some women feel more confident with a doctor, while some feel better with a midwife. Some are more comfortable delivering in a hospital, some at a birthing center or at home. What matters most is your level of confidence in your medical provider. In a moment of crisis or even during a practical discussion, you need to be able to look that person in the eye and feel that she or he is competent and has your best interests at heart.

Having a baby is the most important experience of your life. Plan well and seek out a care provider who shares your philosophies. Many people spend tens of thousands of dollars planning a wedding, and we all know what will happen to a lot of those marriages, right? But you'll have your child and the memory of the pregnancy and birth for a lifetime. So spend a little time and energy investigating your health care options.

How do you find a competent health care team? Word of mouth from friends, colleagues, and family is a great start. But you should also interview your potential care provider. If there's something extremely important to you—not having pain medication or avoiding a cesarean section, for example—definitely bring this up. See if he or she appears defensive or closed minded. Always trust your intuition.

The Differences Between an OB/GYN and a Midwife

An OB/GYN is a medical doctor (M.D.). A Certified Nurse Midwife (C.N.M.) is a Registered Nurse with advanced training and, usually, a master's degree in nursing (M.S.N.). Both are highly trained and certified to manage women's health. This includes obstetrics, well-woman exams, contraception, menopause issues, etc.

The significant difference is that an OB can perform surgery, operative vaginal deliveries, and cesarean sections. He or she also takes care of high-risk pregnancies and gynecological medical problems beyond the scope of a C.N.M.

A C.N.M.'s and an OB's approach to pregnancy can be quite different. C.N.M.s usually see pregnancy as a natural process. End of subject. Physicians see it as a natural process too, but some physicians (not all, by any means) may be slightly tainted by their intense training. The result is that sometimes they are accused of treating pregnancy as a medical condition or "disease."

Many women say that C.N.M.s seem to provide a more relaxed, thoughtful service. And many women like the idea of going to a midwife because the vast majority of midwives are women who have children of their own. MDs generally, although not always, see more patients during the day and thus are often perceived as having a less caring attitude. Some women, though, like the idea of getting care from an actual medical doctor.

It takes an enlightened M.D. (like our Fearless Doc) to see the value of a collaborative practice combining the advantages of both. This means that you will likely be faced with a choice. With a routine pregnancy and delivery, an OB/GYN and a C.N.M. are generally equally competent. For a non-routine pregnancy you will likely need an OB/GYN. Your choice will boil down to how you feel personally about their philosophies and bedside manners and who makes you feel most comfortable and confident.

About Our Team

Besides being parents, Fearless Doc **Stuart Fischbein, OB/GYN, F.A.C.O.G.** and Fearless Midwife **Joyce Weckl, M.S.N., C.N.M.,** each have more than two decades of experience delivering babies and treating pregnant women. **Victoria Clayton** is a health writer and mom. The sections written by Dr. Fischbein and Joyce Weckl are clearly delineated with the title "From the Fearless Doc" or "From the Fearless Midwife." Both authorities have, however, reviewed the entire contents of this book—including the anecdotal advice given by Victoria and her fearless friends—for medical accuracy and sanity.

Fear and You: A Snapshot

Studies in animals and humans have focused on pinpointing the specific brain areas and circuits involved in anxiety and fear. It's been found that the body's fear response is coordinated by a small structure deep inside the brain, called the amygdala.

Neuroscientists have shown that when confronted with a specific fear, your body sends two sets of signals to different parts of the brain. One set of signals, which takes a more roundabout route, relays information to the cerebral cortex, the cognitive (thinking) part of the brain that interprets in detail a threat or fear. The other set of signals shoots straight to the amygdala, which sets the body's physical fear response in motion. This latter effect readies the body for quick action. It causes your heart to pound and diverts blood from the digestive system to the muscles. Stress hormones and glucose flood the blood stream to provide the energy to fight or flee.

Over the long run, fear and anxiety can elevate blood pressure, cause digestive problems, and even suppress the immune system. In the delivery room, fear causes increased tension and anxiety, which can impede relaxation and the process of birth. But the greatest tragedy, we think, is that too many women and their partners are frightened and confused at an important time in their lives when they could be experiencing enormous joy. Living in fear at this momentous time is not really living.

Psychologists tell us that worry and fear are often desensitizing mechanisms that keep us from more powerfully experiencing a situation. Fear brings you up in your head—you think, think, think—and it gets you out of your body. You fear instead of feel. What would real feeling and living do for you and your pregnancy? Think of it this way: A fearful pregnancy is black and white; a fearless pregnancy is in Technicolor.

The Fearless Pregnancy

Here's your first Fearless Fact: Pregnancy doesn't have to be filled with fear.

Consider this: If the reproductive system of humans was so very fragile, we would have been extinct long ago. Pregnancy is a natural function of the female body and, like your other bodily functions, seems to work correctly almost every time. Fetal development, in fact, is amazingly resilient and steadfast, and there is little you encounter in your daily life that can change this. The *Fearless Pregnancy* bottom line is that you need not have a fear of living normally in the twenty-first century. Avoiding behaviors that are obviously dangerous and habits that are excessive is wise, of course, but all it takes is common sense to have a healthy pregnancy. Radiation fallout from a blown nuclear reactor should be avoided, but indicated x-rays or airport metal detectors shouldn't. Smoking two packs of cigarettes a day can have an effect on the growth of your baby, but encountering a few minutes of second-hand smoke a day won't.

Furthermore, it might be encouraging to realize you've already conquered a considerable amount of fear. Before you even became pregnant, there was the fear of deciding that you were going to try to get pregnant. What might happen if you couldn't? For some women, that thought alone stops them from even going off birth control. So pat yourself on the stomach if you've had the courage and faith in humanity to get this far. Of course, you brave woman, it takes a considerable amount of both of these to consciously bring a human being into this world. Now it's time to have a *Fearless Pregnancy.*

The* Fearless Pregnancy *Crib Note Version

When you've finished reading *Fearless Pregnancy,* this is what we want you to come away with: You're special because you're pregnant, but you're not ill. Just live your life normally and with a modicum of common sense and moderation, and the odds that your baby will be born healthy are overwhelmingly good.

2

A Fearless Beginning

"I hate how scared I am to tell people I'm pregnant. What am I scared about? Maybe just that I'll jinx it."
"No pregnancy symptoms today. That makes me nervous; though if something were wrong, I'd probably know it, wouldn't I?"

– From the first-trimester pregnancy journal of Sarah, mother of six-month-old Ash

FEAR: I'll lose the pregnancy.

FEARLESS FACT: Once you see the fetal heartbeat via ultrasound (approximately six weeks from your last period), your chances of miscarriage drop to about 2 percent.

There's one thing that tops the heap of pregnancy fears. I'm just going to come out and say it, although many of you will cringe when you read this word: miscarriage. Almost all newly pregnant women have a fear that they'll lose the baby. It's helpful to realize, though, that misinformation—not medical statistics—plays a large part in how our fear of miscarriage takes root.

If you took a poll, I'm sure you'd find that the majority of people believe there's something magical, for example, about getting beyond the first trimester. Once it's over, many people say, you're out of the miscarriage woods. The truth is better than this. All you really need is twenty-six days from conception to knock your chances of miscarriage down to a measly 2 percent! That's when the fetal heart begins to beat, and when that happens, it's enough to confirm a viable pregnancy has formed.

Twenty-six days from conception usually falls around six weeks from your last period (an easier date to figure). To save heartache, don't consider yourself pregnant until you visit your doctor or midwife at about this time. You'll usually be able to have an early ultrasound and see the heartbeat, although it will only look like a blip of cells. Remember, as soon as you can see the fetal heartbeat on the sonogram, your chances of delivering a real, live baby rise to a reassuring 98 percent.

Learning this was a relief to me in the early stages. It was a stat I used when someone espoused the old "don't tell until after the first trimester" myth. It usually shut that person down, but, more important, it was a number I could hang onto in order to remind myself how much the odds were tipped in my baby's favor.

What's a Sonogram?

"Sonogram" and "ultrasound" are used synonymously for the procedure that allows visual examination of your developing fetus. This technology uses sound waves so high they can't be heard by our human ears, and it carries no risk for your baby or you. A sonogram can be performed through the abdomen (transabdominally) or vagina (transvaginally). Neither is painful. An early sonogram is typically done transvaginally, but subsequent ones will likely be transabdominal.

Does Everyone Get an Early Sonogram?

The American College of Obstetricians and Gynecologists says no ultrasound is *required* if your pregnancy is normal, but most health care providers will do a sonogram around six weeks and another around twenty weeks. You can always request these sonograms if they're not offered. If insurance reimbursement is important (and it is to most people), check with your provider to make sure you're covered.

What Really Causes a Miscarriage?

FEARLESS DOC

Simply put, nature usually does. Early miscarriage—before six weeks—occurs in about 30 percent of all conceptions and at nearly all maternal ages. This is the burden of the human species and is independent of what we do. As sad as we feel at this loss, we can't blame ourselves or fear living normally to try to prevent it. It's both wrong and a bit arrogant to believe we have such power over nature.

Having intercourse, running into a door, or drinking heavily one night before you knew you were pregnant does not cause the miscarriage of a healthy pregnancy or abnormalities in the developing fetus. Some of these activities—ones that cause the uterus to contract—may, in some cases, hasten a miscarriage that would have occurred anyway. This occasionally leaves us to mistakenly believe it was our fault.

Just remember, it isn't the norm of pregnancy to encounter problems. We just hear more about women who do. Our friends share their stories, or we watch too much television. Most often, when a miscarriage occurs, it is important to remember that it is almost never anyone's fault, especially not yours. And there's almost never anything you could have done to prevent it.

Blood Worries?

FEARLESS Midwife

Although I often get phone calls from women panicked about spotting and mild cramping, both are quite common in early pregnancy. Cramping is usually caused by the uterus expanding and is harmless. Spotting, particularly after intercourse or around the time you would have had your period, is likely harmless as well. It's usually due to the placenta growing and attaching. In fact, I've seen women with blood literally running down their legs in the first trimester go on to have normal healthy babies. If you're in doubt, however, or if you're bleeding more heavily than you do during a period and have bad abdominal cramps, call your doctor or midwife for reassurance.

FEARLESS DOC

On those extremely rare occasions when an ultrasound shows a problem or when a woman has heavy bleeding associated with significant cramping and a miscarriage is inevitable, her physician should offer some treatment options. Some women will choose to wait and let everything pass on its own, while others will choose to have a procedure we call a D and C (dilation and curettage). There are pros and cons to both, but here's what is most important: Neither carries any significant risk to your future fertility despite what you may read in any consent form. Listen to your options. Do what seems to make the most sense to you. You can't injure yourself with your choice.

Speak Up!

FEARLESS DOC

When you have concerns about the health of your early pregnancy, be sure to voice those concerns to your partner and to your doctor. Voicing your fears and getting verbal reassurance from those who support you is strong medicine. When necessary, we also can use technology to give you visual reassurance without risk.

FEAR: I don't feel pregnant; maybe something is wrong.

FEARLESS FACT: There's no standard for the way you "feel" when you're pregnant.

Many women have unmistakable symptoms—fairly awful ones for some—in the first trimester, such as breast tenderness, nausea/vomiting, frequent urination, acne, bloating, gas, food cravings/aversions, greasy hair, hair growth, fatigue, and insomnia. All of these are normal and healthy. So too is hardly feeling unusual at all.

My first trimester symptoms were extremely mild—usually nothing an occasional afternoon nap didn't cure. They were so mild, in fact, that when people asked, I found myself saying, "Well, I generally go to the bathroom often anyhow," or "Sometimes I get drowsy around three o'clock even when I'm not pregnant." This could be you too. But don't worry: you have roughly forty weeks, and pretty soon there will be no mistaking that you're pregnant.

Is a Home Pregnancy Test Accurate?

There's something about that simple, relatively cheap home urine test that leaves most people doubting. At least it did me. I've known plenty of friends, too, who don't believe the home tests and wind up making two or three trips to the drug store for new ones.

If you're a doubter, let me give you a tip: buy the two-pack, but not the generic brand. If you buy generic, you're going to doubt the veracity and just go back for the more expensive one anyway. The truth of the home tests, though, is that they're extremely reliable. If one says you're pregnant, you likely are. But before you make any big announcements, see your health care practitioner for an early sonogram.

How Pregnant Are You?

FEARLESS DOC

Accurate dating of pregnancy is one of the most important steps in your prenatal care. Every decision you make and many tests that we run are directly related to or interpreted from where we believe you are in the pregnancy. Using the first day of your last menstrual period as the starting point is the standard convention for dating pregnancies. This is because it's a date most women can recall, whereas the actual date of conception is more nebulous.

It can be confusing, though. For example, an embryo that is twenty-six days from conception would be about forty days from the first day of the last menstrual period for a woman with twenty-eight-day cycles. Therefore, we would call her "almost six weeks," even though she is only almost four. We calculate a "due date" based on 280 days from the first day of your last menstrual period. This is where your practitioner pulls out that crazy wheel to figure it all out. Actually, the normal gestation of a human fetus is 266 days from conception.

Confused yet? The relevance of menstrual dates is that most books use them to discuss the progress of your pregnancy and further divide it into three trimesters. If you get a book on fetal development, however, it will be using actual dates that start with conception.

And, Really, How Pregnant Are You?

When you go in for your first visit, your doctor or midwife will tell you how far along you are. The total pregnancy lasts forty weeks (yep, that's ten, not nine, months). So let's say you're told you're about seven weeks pregnant. Now you'll start obsessing over the count. When are you officially eight weeks? And should you say you're two months pregnant? It's easy to obsess because it's the first question most people will ask you (the second is whether you know the gender). So be prepared.

I got so confused by the weeks and months and by when to change the count that I just decided that each Saturday I would consider myself another week pregnant. I told people how many weeks pregnant I was until six weeks or so before the due date. Then I started saying I had six weeks left, five weeks, etc. It only gets fun when it comes down to the end. I was in Best Buy on my due date, and someone asked me when I was due. Finally, I could say it: "Today!" I loved the shocked look on her face. I guess everybody but you feels more comfortable when you say you have a month left.

Your First Pregnancy Doctor Visit

I saw the positive home pregnancy test on a Sunday, and come nine o'clock Monday, I was on the phone frantically trying to schedule a doctor's appointment. I nearly died when I was told I couldn't get in for another week. But, of course, eventually I got clued in that being pregnant isn't a medical emergency and waiting a week isn't a big deal. In fact, I was fortunate I had to wait, because the timing was perfect.

A home pregnancy test will become positive about ten to fourteen days after conception (about the time you'd expect your next period), but it's wise to wait until six weeks after your last period before you make the doctor's visit. If you go before this, you won't be able to see the fetal heartbeat. Here's what to expect once you do get there:

- A complete health history will be taken. Your practitioner will want to know the first day of your last menstrual period to help determine your due date. If you're like me, you might be a little dazed and confused because you're not yet used to the idea of "being with child," so whip out your calendar while you're at home and try to figure this out in advance. Dating the pregnancy accurately is quite important, so this information will be useful. That said, if your periods are irregular or you just can't pin down the date, don't worry. The exam and early ultrasound will also help date the pregnancy. You'll also be asked to guess your pre-pregnancy weight; it's likely not much less than what you currently weigh. (Note: this is obviously not the time to lie and make your pre-pregnant self skinnier, because then it will just appear that you've gained more during your pregnancy.) You'll also be asked about prescriptions, street drugs, and alcohol and cigarette use. Again, it's not wise to lie, but it's usually not something to fret about either.
- Your weight and blood pressure will be checked.

- An early ultrasound will be done to see the fetal heartbeat and re-confirm the dating of the pregnancy (given that you're at least six weeks from your last period).
- Blood will be drawn to test for type, certain disorders or sexually transmitted diseases, and Rh factor. (If you're needle-phobic, take heart, because you usually will get your blood drawn only three times during the entire pregnancy.)
- A Pap test will be done to look for abnormal cervical cells. (You're not likely to have this, particularly if you've gotten relatively regular Pap smears.)
- Urine will be collected primarily to check for latent urinary tract infections. (Don't worry if you have one, though, because it's easily treated.)
- You'll probably be given written material on healthy eating and prenatal testing. I found it a bit dizzying and basically came home, flopped on the couch, and fell asleep with it. Once I read it, I remained unsatisfied. It seemed like a preposterous diet plan (almost as ridiculous as trying to follow some of those diets you cut out of women's magazines). And some of the information on my testing options was pretty bureaucratic because it came from the state. You should discuss the particulars of your pregnancy with your practitioner on visit number two. And, fortunately, you also have us to help you out.

See also chapter 3, Fearless Prenatal Testing, *for a complete explanation of the tests mentioned above and other prenatal screening tests.*

See also chapter 4, Fearless Diet, Weight Gain, and Exercise, *and chapter 6,* Fearless (Pregnant) Living.

The First Trimester Prenatal Screening

If you're over thirty-five, you may have heard that invasive testing such as the CVS (chorionic villus sampling) and/or an amniocentesis are imperative (see the section on these tests for details).

But hold on. There's another test that may rule out your need for these. It's the first trimester prenatal screening, offered between eleven and fourteen weeks. It's an accurate and excellent noninvasive (that means painless) screening test that involves an ultrasound exam and a blood sample. A report is generated to assess the risk of specific chromosomal abnormalities such as Down syndrome, and the screening will detect about 90 percent of these abnormal pregnancies.

It's important to know that the test isn't definitive, though, so don't make the mistake of thinking a "positive" means something is wrong. It only means more testing—such as the CVS or amnio—is recommended. A "negative" result, however, implies that the risk is less than we might expect and can often reassure those on the fence that further testing probably isn't necessary.

NOTE: Some health plans won't cover this screening test, so check with your insurer before you decide to have it. Most, however, will.

See also chapter 3, Fearless Prenatal Testing, *for more information on first-trimester screening and all other prenatal tests.*

Am I Going to Live at the Doctor's Office Now?

FEARLESS Midwife

When women bring this up, I want to laugh. If you're lucky, in today's managed care environment you'll get fifteen minutes per office visit. We schedule thirty minutes so we have time for chit-chat and questions, but in some HMOs you get about five minutes. Truth be told, though, that's all that's really needed to get business done (save for your questions). So you shouldn't be concerned if your visits seem rather short—as long as you feel you have the opportunity to ask questions and have them answered.

Here's what will happen at your routine first-trimester office visits, which will probably be scheduled once a month until you're twenty-eight weeks and probably won't even require that you undress:

- You'll test your urine for glucose and protein.
- You'll be weighed.
- Your blood pressure will be taken.
- Your practitioner will use a Doppler device to listen to the baby's heartbeat and let you hear it too.
- Your practitioner will externally palpate your uterus to check its size and ensure your baby is growing properly.

For more on glucose and protein testing, see chapter 3, Fearless Prenatal Testing.

FEAR: People are acting so weird. Is something wrong?

FEARLESS FACT: Many people have their own fears about parenthood, and they'll often project them onto *you*.

My husband and I started delivering the news of my pregnancy when I was about seven weeks. We were excited to lay it on family and friends—especially since plenty of people weren't aware that we were trying and most people probably thought we were perfectly content with our dog Celia. I mean, we were one of those obnoxious, canine-obsessed couples; we actually threw a birthday party for Celia (it was tongue-in-cheek; at least I think it was).

When I told family and friends of the pregnancy, I fully expected them to shriek with joy and want to rub my tummy for luck. Of course, many people did that very thing. But there were also a few peculiar reactions, to say the least. I found these strange reactions generally fell into three categories:

1. Naysayers—people who turn ashen and then exclaim, "You're telling people this early?" They usually launch into details of their miscarriage back in 1978.

2. Miscellaneous emotional outbursts/un-PC responses—that is, women who burst into tears or men who say, "How'd it happen? You just…" (followed by a pumping motion using the whole body). Note: It doesn't seem believable, but I swear an otherwise normal neighbor walking his dog in the park said this to me!

3. Vanishing friends—people you consider friends who are suddenly MIA upon news of the pregnancy.

Generally, there are good reasons behind these bizarre reactions and they probably have very little to do with you. For example, the woman who started crying had recently had a hysterectomy. I don't have a good explanation for the

When You Must Deliver Your Good News Gently

Imagine a good friend is struggling with infertility. Now here you are: you barely tried, and you're knocked up. At least, she might see it that way. So how do you approach the subject? It's wise for you to recognize her struggles; otherwise, it'll be the proverbial white elephant in the living room. I didn't do this with one of my old friends, and it was a big mistake.

Here's how to handle it better than I did. Tell her, in person if possible, that you're pregnant. And make sure she's one of the first friends you tell. Then try some version of, "I know you've been struggling to get pregnant, and I'm keeping my fingers crossed that it happens, but I also want you to take part in my pregnancy as much as you feel comfortable." Then you must be okay with whatever happens, even if you don't hear from her until your child's first birthday. On the other hand, don't be shocked if she really wants to be involved. She might even volunteer to throw you a shower or be your backup coach.

neighbor guy, but I'm sure he has one. As for the MIA friends, I later found out that one had endured two unsuccessful in vitro attempts (I knew she wanted a baby and hadn't gotten pregnant yet, but she'd kept the in vitro secret). Another vanishing friend was dealing with a wrecked marriage.

So how do you handle this? The naysayers are easy. Tell them what you learned in the first Fearless Fact. If they are particularly annoying and/or persistent, it can become a "talk to the hand" issue. In other words, just let them know you don't want to hear it. If you're a little rude, that's okay, because most people will cut a pregnant woman some slack. It's also helpful to develop your own "mantra"—an inner saying that you'll use when uninformed people are being annoying or provoking fear. There are several mantras that include four-letter words, or you could just borrow my friend Jane's mantra: Deflect, deflect, deflect.

Miscellaneous unusual responses will just have to be tolerated. Look on the bright side. If someone bursts into tears, it could be that she is just so darn happy for you. Guys in the park? Get away as quickly as possible and let them deal with their own issues by themselves.

The friend thing is a bit stickier. Unfortunately, your pregnancy might require that some of your friends take a break from you. Women in the midst of personal crises like infertility and divorce aren't usually attracted to pregnant women. That's okay. You can deal with this. If you haven't already been where they are, you might be one day, and you'll appreciate having others be gracious when you don't respond to their huge life news as you ought.

Also, realize some of your friends may be feeling left behind. Why? Psychologists say women are geared to look for "ideal sisters" in their friendships. If you're doing something that your sister isn't, she may be afraid you're deserting her for motherhood. She may also be jealous. Try to empathize, try to be the normal you (not the self-absorbed, pregnancy-obsessed you), and then just let them go. They'll probably be back. Besides, the reality is that very soon you'll likely meet a lot of pregnant women and moms. By next year, you could have a whole new crop of friends—if you really need it.

Fast and Fearless

Here's what you need before you start telling people you're pregnant:

1. An early sonogram to confirm the fetal heartbeat (approximately six weeks after conception)
2. No expectations and a large dose of understanding for others
3. A mantra to ward off odd, alarming, or fear-based reactions (try "Deflect, deflect, deflect")

Eat, Drink, and Be Pregnant

FEARLESS DOC

You will be inundated with articles, advertisements, and hearsay from well-meaning friends telling you what to eat and drink and what to avoid. Here's the truth: You can pretty much eat and drink anything as long as it's in moderation. You're not going to get mercury poisoning from having halibut for dinner one night. You won't get parasites from eating sushi at a reputable restaurant. You won't even harm your baby with an *occasional* glass of wine or a daily cup of coffee.

The most important thing is that you eat regularly, about six to seven times a day. Have small amounts every two to three hours and try to eat from the various food groups. If you've had fruits and vegetables all day, make sure you get some protein at the next meal. Eating frequently will keep your blood sugar in a more constant range, which is healthy for your baby, and eating a variety of foods will also ensure that you get a full complement of nutrients.

Whatever you do, don't waste time obsessing about what you eat at any given meal. That's the "special diet" approach and it's confusing, stress-inducing, and simply unnecessary. We aren't so fragile that we need this approach, and neither is that little baby tucked safely away in your womb.

See also chapter 4, Fearless Diet, Weight Gain, and Exercise.

FEAR: Whether I have "morning sickness" or not is indicative of my baby's well-being.

FEARLESS FACT: Whether you're extremely sick or not sick at all is not a predictor of a pregnancy's success or failure.

I was four months pregnant when I got two magazine assignments about what is incorrectly called "morning sickness." I have no idea why it's called this because, as you may have already discovered, this sickness can last all day long. Or, if you're like me, you may *not* have discovered this. Which leads me directly to another first fear you may have as a newly pregnant being.

Morning sickness (the medical term used to refer to extreme forms is *hyperemesis gravidarum*) has become synonymous with pregnancy in our culture. But certainly not every pregnant woman has it! Being nausea-free and pregnant, I rightly thought I was simply lucky. Then I interviewed a woman I'll refer to as the Morning Sickness Queen. The Morning Sickness Queen makes her living counseling pregnant women in person and online. Obviously, she comes into contact with some of the more extreme cases, but she seemed to be on a personal mission to inform the world that morning sickness is a dire problem, contributing greatly to the abortion rate. I don't know about you, but I've never heard of a woman who wanted a child opting to not have hers because of morning sickness.

When I told the Morning Sickness Queen that I wasn't sick at all, she lowered her voice and said, "Oh, please tell me that you were maybe a little queasy a few times." The message she wanted to deliver was that getting sick is good and not getting sick is bad. The truth is, though, only a little more than half of pregnant women are afflicted with nausea.

The Morning Sickness Queen and others like her may come to the sickness-is-good conclusion because researchers—in their valiant efforts, I believe, to make queasy mothers feel better—have launched a theory that pregnancy sickness is the body's natural defense system at work, protecting your babe from harmful toxins. It's easy to jump to the conclusion, then, that if you're not sick, your inane body must not be protecting your child from harmful toxins. But it doesn't work exactly that way. The bottom line is that nobody has concluded that not being sick is a bad sign. If you are not sick, though, you will likely encounter your own Morning Sickness Queen, somebody who erroneously believes it's a bad omen if you aren't vomiting.

To end the tale of the Morning Sickness Queen, I must tell you that almost as an afterthought—with increased worries and fear running around in my pregnant head—I asked her how many children she had. "Who me?" she responded. "I've never had any. I was engaged once and got interested in morning sickness because I thought I might need the information at some point. But we broke off the engagement, and I never married or had children." Right then I made a new rule not to take pregnancy or child-rearing advice from people who have never gone down this road. Instead, I got off the phone and dialed up Jane, who had recently had a healthy baby boy despite never having a moment of being queasy.

Why Do We Get Sick—Or Not?

Nausea hinges on a myriad of factors. The most popular theory about morning sickness is that it's due to elevated hormones, primarily human chorionic gonadotropin and estrogen. Researchers believe that nausea may have to do with the amount of hormones circulating (more means a greater chance you're feeling pukey) and perhaps the structure of certain hormones or your particular sensitivity to them. Also, if you have a pre-pregnancy tendency toward motion sickness, it may mean the area of your brain that controls nausea and vomiting is more sensitive.

Environment can also play a role. Smells such as perfume, dog food, or coffee, as well as motion and the sight of certain foods (one friend would puke at the sight of a can of tuna!) can all trigger nausea. Also, stress, fatigue, and operating on an empty stomach can make you more prone to gastrointestinal upsets.

The bottom line is, nobody really knows why some women get sick and others don't. If you're really sick, you're not going to like hearing this, but the truth is that all the research grants seem to be going to things like diabetes, AIDS, and cancer these days. I don't think there's a ton of hope that we'll ever know the why or why not behind morning sickness.

Home Remedies for Morning Sickness

If you experience morning sickness, you'll be desperate to try anything to calm your stomach. And that's exactly what you should do. Anything that you think might work, no matter how bizarre or nutritionally sinful, is worth a shot. Everyone says it's heartening to remember that morning sickness usually subsides by twelve weeks, but if you're really sick, that's going to feel like a lifetime. Besides, for some women the nausea unfortunately lasts the whole pregnancy, despite the fact that they are healthy and so is the baby. So if vomiting is severe, ask your doctor about prescription medications. They'll definitely decrease the vomiting without risk to your baby or you. (Usually they decrease nausea too, but they can't always eliminate it.)

If you become extremely dehydrated, your doctor may recommend that you be given fluids intravenously, which, again, isn't harmful. But first try these home remedies (the last is my favorite):

- **Ginger.** This root has been used for centuries to fight nausea. Try ginger jam on toast, pickled Chinese ginger, or ginger tea. Ginger ales with real ginger (versus artificial flavorings) may also work. Look for them at health food stores.
- **Lemons.** Sniff them, eat them, or lick them. The refreshing smell and taste calm many women's stomachs. Suck lemon drop candy if fresh lemons aren't available. Lemon air freshener in the car may also help.
- **Acupressure wristbands.** Research conducted in Norway found that 71 percent of a study group of pregnant women who wore acupressure bands reported less intensive sickness and reduced duration of symptoms. Look for Sea Bands or Relief Bands in drug and health food stores.
- **Vitamin B6.** Many years ago, there was a product on the market that actually kicked morning sickness in the butt. It was essentially a combination of the over-the-counter sleep aid Unisom and plain, old vitamin B6. It was said to work superbly, although the manufacturers ceased making it because of some legal wrangling. This combination does not sound like anything most pregnant women think they can take, but guess what? You can. If you're real sick, ask your doctor about trying 50 milligrams of vitamin B6 a day.
- **Consult your food fairy.** If you could eat anything, what would it be? Even if it's waffles and brownie sundaes, go for it. Many women are determined

to do nutritional overhauls when they find out they're pregnant, but even dietitians say the real key when you're sick is to eat anything as long as you can keep it down. Any food will protect your stomach lining and prevent low blood sugar (which can exacerbate nausea). I'm personally quite fond of the health food store, but even I say that if you're sick, pregnant or not, and McNuggets make you feel better, order the twenty-piece pack. There's plenty of time for nutritional virtue when you're well.

What Happens If You Can't Stomach Your Prenatal Vitamin?

FEARLESS Midwife

I often have patients who are excessively nauseated and, because of it, excessively worried. They think that they must be suffering because of their nutritional failures. If this is you, realize that even if you vomit through your entire first trimester or if the only things you can stomach are potato chips and Coke, your baby will not suffer because of it.

Babies are like little leaches. They'll pull from your body what they need. They don't even need much in the beginning, because most of this first trimester your baby is smaller than your thumbnail. Even if you can't stomach your prenatal vitamins, you needn't worry. The most important nutrient in the prenatal vitamin for the first trimester is folic acid. If you have a lot of vomiting and can't stomach your vitamins, just buy a folic acid 400-microgram supplement and take that twice a day.

~ *Fast and Fearless*

Here's what you need to know about morning sickness:

1. Don't be scared about excessive nausea or none at all. Neither is an indicator of the viability of your pregnancy, and neither will harm your baby.
2. If you get sick, forget about sound nutrition and just eat whatever you can keep down. Also, consider the brighter side—use the sickness to get out of bothersome household chores like feeding the dog, cleaning, or cooking.
3. Morning sickness usually stops after the first trimester, but if it's persistent and/or severe, ask your doctor to prescribe antiemetics, which are perfectly safe.

S-E-X?

If you want to have it, have it. That's the rule for any routine pregnancy. There's nothing you can do—unless you plan to hang from a chandelier and fall—that will hurt your baby.

For more, see also chapter 6, *Fearless (Pregnant) Living.*

FEAR: I'm becoming a bitch.

FEARLESS FACT: You're developing into a lioness.

No matter what your age, being pregnant is the first time many women feel like real adults. I know, we should all feel like real adults when we hit eighteen, but there's something about the idea of being someone's mother that, unlike being able to vote, seals the deal for many of us. Impending motherhood causes interesting changes in many women's attitudes.

As my niece Jennifer put it, once she discovered she was pregnant, she also discovered she had a set of *cajones.* A big and growing set. She became very straightforward and decisive at work, with salespeople, etc. Perhaps this is Mother Nature's way of balancing that big and growing set of breasts, but more than likely any increased assertiveness (and perhaps, yes, we can even call this bitchiness) is due to a mix of hormonal changes and the new psychological weight of motherhood. If you're being extremely assertive, maybe you're practicing bossing people around as you imagine you'll need to boss your kid around. The truth is that a year from now, you'll be too tired and too humbled to roar. So enjoy it while you can.

Roller-Coaster Moods?

Many pregnant women are bitchy one minute and tearful the next. In fact, it was bossy Jennifer who also teared up because the local mall changed its name! There's nothing wrong with you; it's just hormones. Women with a tendency toward premenstrual moodiness are especially prone to pregnancy mood shifts. When you're on a nice swing, appeal to friends and family to try to understand. But most people—even strangers—already realize pregnant women can be a little testy and/or sensitive.

FEAR: I'm going to become my mother.

FEARLESS FACT: You're going to be better than—and have more in common with—your mother.

It's typical for women, when they find out they're pregnant, to worry about the kind of mother they'll be. More to the point, we worry we'll become our mothers, whether that means smothering, neglectful, or something else. (If you're among the .00001 percent of women who've been blessed to have a supportive, loving, intelligent, witty, socially acceptable, perfect mother, I grant you a free pass to skip this section.)

It's good to keep in mind that you're not *becoming* your mother. In many respects, you already are her. You share her genetic makeup and/or years of environmental influence. There's simply nothing you can do to erase this. Luckily, however, you can improve upon it. Start reading up on parenting issues. It's a great activity to pursue instead of obsessing about your pregnancy. This gives you a chance to really think about how you were mothered and to develop your own—hopefully improved—parenting philosophies. Keep in mind, too, that your mother also felt these fears.

FEAR: We're going to go broke!

FEARLESS FACT: In many cases there's help available, and besides, having a baby may not be quite as expensive as you think.

More and more women are self-employed these days, and that means more of us are responsible for our own health insurance. Also, many working women are employed by companies that no longer provide health insurance. And even those of us who are covered may be fearful that our part of the financial burden will be substantial. I know I was. Here's how to handle money concerns:

- If you are currently insured, call the member services department of your health plan and inquire about your maternity coverage. I was pleasantly surprised to find that my insurance company, Blue Cross, had recently made it less of a penalty to have a baby by eliminating a $1,500 maternity deductible. We were still responsible for several thousand dollars worth of care in the end, but finding out what your benefits are will help you prepare.
- Armed with the knowledge of what your plan covers, speak with your practitioner's office manager. The office manager should be able to give you a rough idea of your total cash cost. If you truly can't afford this sum, your practitioner may offer special payment arrangements or even a discount. Many hospitals also offer substantial discounts if you make arrangements ahead of time.
- If you become pregnant while you're uninsured, don't panic. You probably have more options than you might imagine. It's true that pregnancy is a pre-existing condition, making it difficult, if not impossible, to apply for the typical health plan. But that's also just as well, because usually there are

better options. Lower-income women will qualify for free prenatal and newborn care. And in most states there are special affordable insurance plans for middle-income women who are pregnant. Ask your health care practitioner or call Planned Parenthood for advice on where to turn.

- Also, while it may be fun to raid Babies R Us for a roomful of special gizmos for the baby, the truth is that much of it is unnecessary and/or designed to appeal to naïve/scared new moms. Often, women with older children come out of the woodwork and give you tons of truly useful gear and clothes. So if money is a problem, save yours for diapers (you will need those and they can get expensive) and buy gadgets only when you really need them.

For more tips, see also chapter 7, Fearless Gear Buying.

~ *Fast and Fearless*

Here's all you really need to know for a fearless first trimester:

- There's very little you can do to cause a miscarriage, so don't waste precious time fearing it.
- Spotting and mild cramping are very common and usually not bad signs.
- Don't watch too many scary deliveries on television.
- Expect to experience every emotion, from fear to exaltation to hostility. It will all be there.
- Take a home pregnancy test and do believe the results, but wait until you have the six-week vaginal ultrasound and see a heartbeat before you make the big announcement.
- Tell everyone—even strangers—after you see the heartbeat. If you look green and act ferocious, at least they'll know why. Perhaps they'll cut you some slack.
- Morning sickness can last all day. Having it and not having it are both normal and indicate nothing about the viability of your pregnancy, despite what *anyone* says.
- Don't obsess over what you eat and drink. You can have most things, as long as you practice moderation.

- Regarding your big announcement, be prepared for fallout. Announcing a pregnancy can trigger intensely emotional responses from loved ones and strangers. Practice your ability to separate yourself from any bizarre or fear-inducing reactions.
- Instead of obsessing about your pregnancy, consider obsessing over parenting. That situation lasts longer, and the payoff for being prepared will likely be greater.
- If you're uninsured or financially shaky, talk to your practitioner's office manager and/or call a women's health clinic or Planned Parenthood. There's help available for every pregnant woman.

3

Fearless Prenatal Testing

"The fear I had about testing, and particularly the amniocentesis, was from hearing other mothers make more of it than it was. In truth, it wasn't that big of a deal."

– Jane, mother of one-year-old Simba

3

Fearless Prenatal Testing

"The fear I had about testing, and particularly the amniocentesis, was from hearing other mothers make more of it than it was. In truth, it wasn't that big of a deal."

– Jane, mother of one-year-old Simba

First Trimester Tests

- Early ultrasound
- Routine blood tests
- Urine analysis
- Pap smear and vaginal cultures
- Chorionic villus sampling* *(placental biopsy and ultrasound)*
- First trimester prenatal screen* *(blood test and ultrasound)*
- Genetic counseling* *(may include blood test)*

Second Trimester Tests

- Genetic ultrasound
- Routine blood tests
- AFP/triple marker blood test
- Quadruple marker prenatal screening
- Diabetes screening
- Amniocentesis* *(amniotic fluid sample and ultrasound)*

Third Trimester Tests

- Group B strep vaginal/rectal culture
- Nonstress test/biophysical profile*
- Stress test* *(contraction test)*

* *Indicates tests that are performed as required or are perhaps requested for your pregnancy. All other tests are generally performed in all pregnancies.*

From the Fearless Doc:

Some Answers About Tests

What's a Chorionic Villus Sampling (CVS)?

Performed between ten and twelve weeks into a pregnancy, this procedure involves having a specialist called a perinatologist take a small sampling (biopsy) of the placental material, which is sent for analysis. This material comes from the same fertilized egg as the developing fetus and, therefore, contains the same genetic material. That means results are definitive.

CVS is usually used to detect Down syndrome but may also be used to pick up sickle cell anemia, cystic fibrosis, Tay-Sachs, and a few other disorders if there's a family history. It doesn't test for neural tube (that is, spinal column) defects. In proper hands, this procedure carries a risk of miscarriage of about 1 in 300. There is very little discomfort, although there may be some light bleeding, and the results are available quickly—usually within three days.

What's a Perinatologist?

This highly trained physician has taken a fellowship in the high-risk specialty called Maternal-Fetal Medicine. You'll meet one if you have a CVS, are having multiple births, or are considered at high risk for any variety of reasons.

What's a First Trimester Prenatal Screen?

Performed between eleven and fourteen weeks, this procedure is one in which a blood sample is analyzed and an ultrasound is performed. The test is helpful at detecting Down syndrome (Trisomy 21) and Trisomy 18, the two most common age-related chromosomal abnormalities. It measures the level of two hormones called free beta-hCG and PAPP-A.

During the ultrasound, an area of the fetus' neck is measured. The two reports are then used to re-assess the risk of Trisomy 21 and 18. The blood test doesn't include a biochemical screen for small neural tube defects, but because the ultrasound is so accurate, the doctor or ultrasonographer will also look for this abnormality. This is a painless, noninvasive test that's very good, but it's not iron-clad. A positive result doesn't mean your baby is abnormal; it does mean, however, your practitioner will probably recommend an amniocentesis.

What's an AFP/Triple Marker Screening?

Performed between fifteen and twenty weeks, this test involves sending a blood sample to a lab that measures levels of three markers—AFP, hCG, and estriol—in your blood. The test is helpful in detecting neural tube defects such as spina bifida (failure of the fetus's neural tube to close properly). A normal value is highly predictive of no abnormality. An abnormal value simply means you're a candidate for more testing.

Prior to the newer first trimester prenatal screen, the AFP/triple marker was used to screen for neural tube defects as well as Down syndrome. In many parts of the country, it's still the most widely available screening test. Its positive predictive value of a normal baby isn't as good as the first trimester prenatal screen, however, and it tends to have slightly more false positives, which often lead to anxiety and further invasive tests such as amniocentesis. For this reason, if you can get a first trimester prenatal screen and it comes back normal, I recommend skipping the AFP/triple marker and asking for a genetic ultrasound at around eighteen to twenty weeks.

What's a Quadruple Marker Prenatal Screen?

This is a new addition to the screening arsenal. A fourth biochemical substance called inhibin-A is added to the triple marker screen and provides for greater sensitivity in screening for Trisomy 21 or Trisomy 18. This means that a negative test is more likely to predict a chromosomally normal baby and there are fewer false positives. The quad screen is a blood test performed between the 15th and 20th week just like the triple marker. Ask your practitioner if it is available in your area.

What's an Amniocentesis?

For this test, usually performed between fourteen and sixteen weeks, a physician, using ultrasonic guidance, passes a thin needle through the skin of your lower abdomen into the sac of fluid surrounding your baby. This fluid contains cells with genetic material and analysis of the cells is roughly 99.9 percent accurate for detecting Down syndrome. (Testing for other genetic abnormalities may also be done.) The fluid is sent to a laboratory, which has the results in seven to twenty-one days. Because the cells need to be grown in a tissue culture, there is a wide variation in the time it takes for results to return. *There is absolutely no correlation between how long it takes for your results to come back and the normality or abnormality of those results.*

In well-trained hands, this procedure takes a mere twenty seconds and involves minimal discomfort. I've found that the emotional anxiety leading up to the test is far worse than the test itself. Most amnios are performed because the mother is over thirty-five, although age alone isn't necessarily the best reason to get one. A family history of genetic problems, a positive first trimester prenatal screen, or a positive AFP/triple marker are better reasons.

What's a Genetic Ultrasound?

Performed at around eighteen to twenty weeks, this test provides a detailed survey of the baby's anatomy. With this test, we can rule out most major anatomic defects, including spina bifida, and can look for any evidence of more subtle ones.

The ultrasound records echoes of sound waves as they bounce off parts of the fetus, and then translates the echoes into a picture. Your doctor may have to point out various parts of the body, but even an untrained eye can see the head and limbs. The newest ultrasounds offer computerized 3-D images that are incredibly clear. Some can even estimate the baby's current weight.

The location of the placenta as well as abnormalities or, most likely, a lack of abnormalities in your uterus and ovaries will also be observed. If you want, you can videotape the exam; it's exciting to see the baby move, swallow, and sometimes yawn. When this final test is concluded, you can take a deep breath, rid yourself of that universal fear that something might be wrong with your baby, and get on with enjoying your pregnancy!

What's a Nonstress Test/Biophysical Profile?

A nonstress test is simply a fetal heart monitor that records the pattern of your baby's heartbeat over a period of time, usually twenty to thirty minutes. We look for patterns we know to be reassuring.

Often the nonstress test is enhanced by a test called a "biophysical profile." This means that a short ultrasound is also added. During the ultrasound, we check for four additional parameters: amniotic fluid level, fetal movement, fetal tone (the flexed position of the baby's limbs, which coordinates closely with fetal movement), and fetal "breathing."

You'll usually have this test only if you're overdue, detect a decrease in fetal movement, develop diabetes or high blood pressure, have abnormal bleeding, show poor fetal growth, or are having multiple births.

What's a Stress Test?

Also called a "contraction stress test," this may be used when results from a nonstress test aren't reassuring. Usually, however, if the biophysical profile (see above) indicates a potential problem, the baby will be delivered. If a stress test is ordered, a drug called Pitocin will be given to you by i.v. to stimulate contractions. The fetal heart rate is then monitored to see how the baby deals with the stress of the contractions. Three contractions in ten minutes are the desired goal. A nonreassuring pattern means your baby should be delivered. Again, with the increased reliance on the biophysical profile, this test is used far less frequently today.

At Every Doctor Visit...

On each and every visit, you'll have prenatal tests of some sort. You'll get your weight and blood pressure measured and have your urine checked. Here's why...

WEIGHT:

Ahhh, it gets a little painful as the numbers creep up, but the rule is you never have to tell anyone how much you've gained, even though some people will definitely ask. Tell them your doc says you're the perfect weight. Your weight gain is being checked to monitor your baby's health and your health. You want to grow, of course; that's what it's all about. But if your weight skyrockets and you haven't been eating truckloads of food, your practitioner will know there may be a problem worthy of investigation.

See also chapter 4, Fearless Diet, Weight Gain, and Exercise.

BLOOD PRESSURE:

This is pleasant because you don't have to disrobe and nobody is poking around anywhere. It's necessary because it can give your doctor an early warning of pregnancy-induced hypertension or preeclampsia. But don't worry, because that condition is pretty rare and is readily treated when caught early.

URINE:

By the end of the pregnancy, you'll become a pro at peeing in a cup and using a dipstick to check your own urine for sugar and protein. You'll just automatically let yourself in the bathroom and do your test as if you're a real, live medical professional. In that way, it's sort of fun. Otherwise, it's uneventful.

Of course, if you have a particularly high-service doctor, perhaps a nurse will do this for you (not pee for you, but test your urine)! But, then again, that takes away all the fun. Normally, there will be no sugar in your urine, but I'm told a very small amount is acceptable, especially after eating. Protein in your urine will also likely be negative. If you have protein in your urine, it may be an early sign of preeclampsia. If you repeatedly have large amounts of sugar in your urine, your practitioner will check you early for pregnancy-induced diabetes.

See also The Diabetes Test, *page 70.*

FEAR: I'm over thirty-five, so I'll be required to have a gazillion tests.

FEARLESS FACT: Age is only one factor—and not even the biggest one—in determining your baby's risk of genetic abnormalities. Besides, tests are optional.

I was thirty-five when I became pregnant, and right away I thought an amniocentesis was mandatory. I'd sat through an amnio with my friend Donna a few years earlier and had thought, as an observer, that it didn't seem half as bad as what I'd heard about it. Donna also confirmed that it wasn't painful or in any way truly horrible. Still, what I didn't realize was that just because I was thirty-five didn't mean this test was essential.

In a discussion with my doctor and midwife, I was told that since there wasn't a family history of genetic problems, they saw little need for the amnio if my AFP/triple marker screening came back negative and I felt okay about not having it. The screening did come back negative (although a better option is actually to get the first trimester prenatal screening blood test, which is even more accurate). I opted *not* to get the amnio because of this. Donna, on the other hand, said she felt better with the more accurate results from the amnio. My friend Jane, who was forty when she got pregnant, also opted for the amniocentesis. She decided any information she could get on the baby was a good thing (the happy results gave her and her partner James a heap of reassurance too).

> Statistically, your risk of having a baby with Down syndrome at age thirty-five is one in 286, which means there is a 99.65 percent chance that your baby will not have it.

Jane's and Donna's solution to not feeling at risk with the procedure was to get the amnio done by a doctor who specializes in doing them. The doctors they went to do amnios all day long and have great track records. That seems to be standard advice. If you opt for invasive testing (CVS or amniocentesis), you want to get it done by the local ace, who may be your own provider or a specialist in your area. But, alas, also know that it's outdated to think your age is the only thing that determines your need for genetic testing. Whether you need genetic testing (CVS, amnio, or genetic counseling/testing) also depends upon your health and your own and your partner's family histories.

See also Ding! Ding! Routine Testing, *page 64, and* Genetic Testing, *page 72.*

You're More Than Just Your Age...

FEARLESS DOC

Many of you will have heard that once a woman reaches the age of thirty-five, she must have genetic tests or, at the very least, an amniocentesis. This number was based on some fuzzy math that equated the risk of a chromosomal abnormality such as Down syndrome with the risk of miscarriage from the amniocentesis procedure. The thinking is no longer appropriate and never considered the individuality of all women. You can forget this blanket recommendation.

Instead, talk to your health care provider. He or she will take into account your age, health status, and family history and make recommendations for which tests you might consider.

To Test or Not to Test?

FEARLESS Midwife

Some women say they don't want any tests at all, although I recommend all the routine tests, the AFP/triple marker or first trimester prenatal screen, and the ultrasounds. I realize that some pregnant women just want to be happy and full of hope for the future; they don't want to know anything bad if there's anything bad to know. We can all empathize with this, but in the big picture it's probably not the most responsible way to parent. Being fearless doesn't mean being clueless. It means having adequate information and making choices based on that.

FEAR: My test(s) will be wrong.

FEARLESS FACT: Tests are designed to work, and, overwhelmingly, most do.

The truth of the matter is that, yes, sometimes tests come back either falsely positive or falsely negative. Usually, though, they're pretty accurate. People don't like to mess with the minds of pregnant women, so the screening tests wouldn't be in wide use if they weren't fairly good.

Also, keep in mind that most tests are designed as such: when the test carries a lot of weight (that is, indicates a problem with the baby) and comes back positive, you'll be subjected to further, more accurate testing to get more information. Oftentimes, with the more advanced testing, it'll be determined that the first results were "false positives." A false positive is when the screening test comes up positive but further testing concludes you don't have the problem.

My friend Renee was the queen of false positives during her second pregnancy. She was subjected to a gamut of tests and what she calls "every conceivable diagnosis." She was fraught with worry, as most women would be. The result was that she delivered a healthy boy with absolutely no problems, and he is now six years old and a budding gymnast. Renee remains suspicious

Interpreting Numbers: What Kind of Fish Are You?

Since *Finding Nemo* was such a popular movie—and since lots of kid-friendly movies are in your future—let's use this illustration. If someone tells you the chance of a negative event occurring is one in two hundred, how do you look at it? You could be a Marlin fish and see a significant risk. Or you could be a Dory fish and see a 99.5 percent chance of the event not occurring. See, the same numbers have drastically different meanings to different people—or fish. Do your best to think like Dory.

that her doctors were milking her insurance plan. It's probably not true (have you seen the discounted rates insurance companies have negotiated with doctors?), but the bottom line is that just because a screening test comes back positive doesn't necessarily mean you have a problem. It likely means you'll just get more tests.

What's a Screening Test?

FEARLESS DOC

Only the CVS and amniocentesis tests are definitive. Everything else is a "screening test." Think of screening tests like the metal detector at the airport. A positive "beep" at the metal detector doesn't mean that you get arrested. It only means that further testing is necessary.

What about False Negatives?

FEARLESS Midwife

It's extremely rare to hear of "false negatives." Why? Because regardless of tests and results, the overwhelming majority of babies are born A-OK. Since only a small number of babies are born with problems, the likelihood that you'll test negative for something and have it is minuscule.

Biology 101: Chromosomes and Genes

FEARLESS DOC

I have often found that many patients don't know the difference between a chromosome and a gene. All cells in our body, except sperm and eggs, contain forty-six chromosomes. We receive twenty-three chromosomes from our mother and twenty-three from our father. On these chromosomes are thousands of genes carrying the specifics that make us who we are.

Imagine forty-six ladders lined up across the street. It would be easy to tell if there were one missing, an extra one, or a large piece in the wrong place. These ladders represent your chromosomes. What you may not be able to tell by looking at those ladders is if there is a crack in one of the rungs or steps. These rungs in the ladder represent the genes.

Routine screening for chromosomal defects, the most common of which is Down syndrome, is extremely accurate at telling you there are a normal number of chromosomes. What it can't tell you is that the information on the chromosomes is sound. For that reassurance, the best we have right now is a good family history.

FEAR: My cousin has Down syndrome, and I'm worried these genetic abnormalities will be passed on to my baby.

FEARLESS FACT: Down syndrome is rarely inherited.

This was my friend Anne's worry: since her cousin has Down syndrome, the genetic roulette wheel was going to stop on her baby. I've heard other friends say the same thing.

People also throw around the phrase "skipping a generation." Skipping a generation means your grandparent has something, your parent doesn't, and you do. So it doesn't make too much sense when you bring less direct relatives (such as cousins) into the picture. What I really think these people are saying is that they're frightened they're a "carrier" of a disorder. Most important, realize that only a very rare form of Down syndrome is inherited. The story is the same for mental retardation. Also, know that there's a solution to your worry.

The best thing to do is speak with your doctor and explain your family background in as much detail as possible. He or she may also refer you to a genetic counselor to get more information. Usually, you'll be told that you have no greater odds than anyone else of having a baby born with the same disorder your

Detectable Genetic Diseases

Many genetic diseases can now be identified with blood tests performed on both parents to look for those who might be carriers of a disorder. Every year, there are new discoveries into our genetic makeup, leading to new tests for specific genetic diseases. Common ones we can now screen for include:

- Cystic fibrosis
- Tay-Sachs disease
- Muscular dystrophy
- Fragile X
- Sickle cell disease
- Hemophilia

On Mothers, Mothers-in-Law, and More

Remember that many of the tests now performed during pregnancy weren't around a decade ago, let alone thirty years ago. If your mother or mother-in-law is driving you nuts because she's worried, take some time to tell her about the newfangled tests we now have, or recommend she read up on them.

One of my relatives was having twins, and each and every test came back reassuring, yet her mother was a bag of nerves and voiced her worry at every chance. Finally, the mother was given a book explaining the tests and then invited along on the OB and perinatologist visits just so she'd understand how well everything was going—and shut up! It sort of worked—definitely better than doing nothing.

cousin has (or other relatives, for that matter). There are also tests, such as the first trimester prenatal screen, CVS, AFP/triple marker, ultrasounds, and amniocentesis, all of which can be used to gain reassuring information.

I should warn you, though, that some women, despite what I've just told you, continue to worry. Anne, who is now earning her Ph.D. in chemistry, was steeped in science and still fretted, not because it was reasonable and sane, but because she let superstition and anxiety get the best of her. If this is you, look for the section in this book on fear-fighting exercises. Anne says she wishes she'd known about these, because her son, of course, was just fine, and the increased worry only made her enjoy her pregnancy less. (Some people, I swear, really do enjoy it, but don't worry if you don't exactly; that's normal too.)

What Is a "Carrier"?

A carrier is someone who is normal but harbors a recessive gene. A rough way to look at it is that if two carriers of the same recessive gene conceive a baby, there's a one in four chance that the baby will be seriously affected.

Through all this, remember that most babies are born perfect, which is quite a miracle when you consider how complex we are. Isn't it amazing that one fertilized cell can go on to differentiate into neurons and toenails, retina and nose hairs? That's really what I tell my patients to concentrate on—all that goes right consistently, not all that can go wrong.

What Is Genetic Counseling?

FEARLESS DOC

Occasionally, some couples will be good candidates for genetic counseling. I usually refer patients to a genetic counselor when there's a disorder in their family background that may be inherited and they're concerned.

Genetic counselors specialize in determining the risk for an inherited disorder. Both parents meet with the counseling specialist and offer as much family medical history as possible. The interesting thing is that often this is as far as it goes. The genetic counselor usually puts the couple's fears to rest by informing the parents-to-be that, based on the genetic history they've given, the odds their baby will be born with a certain defect are quite slim.

In some cases, though, blood will be drawn from each parent and sent to a lab for analysis. This is to determine if a parent carries a certain recessive gene. If both parents carry the recessive gene, the chances that the baby will be born with the disorder may be greater, and it will likely be recommended that the fetus be tested as well. Again, the odds that this will happen aren't huge. And many genetic disorders have different mathematical chances of being passed along. That's the genetic counselor's job—to determine your odds. Usually the session is extremely reassuring.

Get What You Need

Nobody can be screened for everything, and legitimate testing is often expensive. Insurance companies, especially HMOs, may not even agree that a test is necessary. Translation: They may not pay. Whether you're covered by insurance or not, it is ultimately your decision and your responsibility to determine what's best for you. If you feel you need the test, get it and then deal with your insurance company later to get payment. Usually, with a little fight, you can ultimately get the insurance company to pay, because it's very bad PR to snub a pregnant woman.

For Over-Thirty-five Mothers

Maybe there should be a target on our backs with the words "I'm over thirty-five and I'm pregnant!"—because that's the way a lot of us, um, "older" mothers feel. Of course, everyone knows that it's extremely common to be over thirty-five and pregnant nowadays. Just this week I found out two women I know are pregnant. One is thirty-six and the other thirty-seven.

A lot of the fear over-thirty-five mothers feel has to do with the extra tests and increased risk of chromosomally abnormal babies. But this risk doesn't suddenly happen when the clock strikes midnight on your thirty-fifth birthday. The truth is, it gradually increases from your early twenties on. Thirty-five was an age arbitrarily chosen before we had sound testing. Besides, nowadays we know that the parents' health, family background, and, yes, age all have to be weighed to determine the risk of delivering a baby who has a problem. Everyone is different, and each woman must discuss her situation with her doctor or midwife.

On the other hand, maybe you're not afraid your baby will have a problem, but you are nervous that you're too old to go through the delivery or even be a mother. My friend Kathryn was forty-two when she had her son Jon. With the help of her reassuring team of midwives, she finally came to the conclusion that if her body could get pregnant, then she could sustain, deliver, and raise a baby just fine. Basically, Kathryn says the mother of all mothers, Mother Nature, deserves some credit for knowing what she's doing.

I think that's a very sane way to look at it. So surround yourself with a health care team that reassures you the way Kathryn's did, and then forget about your age.

What about the Older Daddy?

There's some evidence that a father over the age of fifty-five could contribute to chromosomal problems. But, again, chromosomal abnormalities are really quite rare in any pregnancy.

FEAR: The CVS and/or amniocentesis will cause me to miscarry.

FEARLESS FACT: Your risk is around 0.3 percent.

Numerous studies of the more invasive tests have evaluated the risk of miscarriage, but it's usually about one in five hundred for an amniocentesis and one in three hundred for CVS. That works out to 0.3 percent overall—or, in other words, a 99.7 percent chance that all will go well. And, by the way, the risk isn't that the CVS biopsy or the amnio needle will harm the fetus. The risk is mostly from developing an infection. It has nothing to do with what you do or don't do, though. It's a risk we take when we have almost any invasive medical procedure.

To minimize the chance of a problem, prior to the CVS you'll have cultures done to try to ensure that undesirable bacteria aren't present. And, of course, careful sterile technique is employed in both procedures.

After you have either procedure, you may have light spotting or mild cramping. Don't panic; just take it easy. Call your practitioner if you need reassurance or if your bleeding is heavy. Your CVS results will come back in about three days, but your amnio results will take seven to twenty-one days. Remember, don't be superstitious; the time it takes has nothing to do with the results.

Previous Uterine Surgery

Women who've had previous uterine surgery, such as that for fibroid tumors, are at *slightly* greater risk of infection from an amniocentesis, because scarring or adhesions of the intestine can harbor bacteria that can be introduced by the amnio needle. Still, your risk remains minuscule—almost a 99.7 chance of not having a problem.

CVS Versus Amniocentesis

FEARLESS DOC

Patients who decide further genetic testing is right for them often ask which tests they should have. Here's what I tell my patients: If you carry a known genetic disorder that can be detected by the test, if you have a previously affected child, or if you're fearful that something may be wrong based on an ultrasound or your intuition, choose the CVS procedure. I believe the earlier diagnosis and rapid results, along with the peace of mind they provide, overcome the slight increase in the risk of miscarriage. Again, we are talking about a very small number of complications. Also, choosing this procedure makes termination, if you choose that, technically easier and safer than it would be later in your pregnancy. If, however, you have a more optimistic viewpoint and are having this procedure for routine, age-related concerns or reassurance, then choose amniocentesis.

FEAR: I crave sweets; maybe I'm diabetic.

FEARLESS FACT: Diet can be used to control gestational diabetes, but what you eat has nothing to do with whether you have diabetes.

Only a small percentage of pregnant women develop pregnancy-related (gestational) diabetes, and it has nothing to do with what you eat or what you crave. It has to do with hormones (see what the Fearless Doc has to say about diabetes).

Even if you do have gestational diabetes, be aware that treatment usually involves dietary changes and nutritional counseling. Yes, you probably will have to lay off the sweets, but rarely will insulin be required. And the outcome of a diabetic pregnancy is almost always good with proper care.

By the way, unlike real diabetes, this form of diabetes goes away when you deliver the baby.

See also The Diabetes Test, *page 70.*

The Lowdown on Real Diabetes Versus Gestational Diabetes

FEARLESS DOC

Diabetes is caused by the failure of your pancreas to produce adequate amounts of insulin in response to a rise in the blood sugar level after eating. Insulin is a hormone that acts to maintain your blood sugar in a range that is physiologically useful and desirable for the organs of your body to function properly. When sugars run high over long periods of time (years), it can cause permanent damage to and malfunctions of your kidneys, eyes, circulation, and nervous system. This form of diabetes is often called Type 1 or juvenile-onset because it begins when we are young and is treated by replacing the insulin by injection or pump. Type 2 diabetes is called adult-onset diabetes and has a strong link with obesity.

Gestational diabetes is very different from these true forms of diabetes in that it is only temporary, disappearing after your baby is delivered. Placental hormones, reducing your body's sensitivity to your own insulin, cause gestational diabetes. When the placenta is removed after birth, the process resolves. It doesn't imply that you will someday become diabetic or that anything is wrong with your baby. The most important thing to do if you are told of this diagnosis is to comply with your recommended diet. (You'll likely be put on the American Diabetes Association diet and have to monitor your blood sugar.) Follow the instructions given. You will have a healthy baby.

See also The Diabetes Test, *page 70.*

From the Fearless Midwife:

Ding! Ding! Routine Testing: Get Ready for Three Rounds

As soon as a woman sees a positive pregnancy test result, she immediately rushes to the phone to call the office to schedule an appointment. All women seem to think they need to come in immediately to have their blood drawn. We must pick this up from television, because the truth is that for a routine pregnancy, there's no rush.

You'll likely have three rounds of routine testing during your pregnancy, which include blood work, a Pap smear, a glucose test, urine tests, and, lastly, a vaginal/rectal culture. Each visit you'll also have your blood pressure and weight taken and your urine checked for sugar and protein. (See also *At Every Doctor Visit,* page 52.) These results give us information about your health that can influence your baby's health.

For the majority of women, the tests come back completely fine. And if you test positive for something—a urinary tract infection, for example—you'll be treated, and it won't interfere with the pregnancy.

In addition to this routine testing, you may also opt for some genetic testing, which checks for chromosomal abnormalities of the developing fetus.

See also Genetic Testing, *page 72.*

Routine Testing: Round One

(your first pregnancy appointment)

Once you get in for your first prenatal appointment, you'll immediately encounter a battery of tests. You'll have blood drawn and a vaginal exam. Some of the required testing may vary from state to state, but most are similar.

Having your first round of tests is your first taste of anticipation. Between the time it's done and the time the results come back, many women read up on all the things that might be "wrong." Don't drive yourself nuts! Here's what's being checked and why you probably have very little to worry about:

THE BLOOD PANEL

Test: Blood type and Rh factor

Tells: Your blood type (O, A, B, or AB) and your Rh (positive or negative). You will get a result such as O positive or A negative.

Fearless Fact: The only problem that could possibly exist is handled easily. That is, if you're Rh negative and the father of the baby is Rh positive, your baby may be Rh positive. In this case, you'll simply get a shot of Rhogam when you're twenty-eight weeks pregnant and a smaller dose of Rhogam after an invasive testing such as a CVS or amniocentesis. Rhogam prevents your body from developing antibodies should the baby's blood be incompatible with yours (Rh positive).

Test: Antibody screen

Tells: If your blood has developed antibodies (a.k.a. Pac Man) to any foreign substances

Fearless Fact: Some antibodies indicate a problem and some don't. Rest assured, the ones that indicate a problem are very rare. When this does happen, the pregnancy will need to be followed closely, and you'll be referred to a high-risk specialist.

Antibodies and Rh Factors

An antibody is essentially the Pac Man of your blood. Antibodies gobble up foreign invaders. How does this come into play with Rh negative moms? If you're Rh negative, it means you don't have the "Rh factor" on your red blood cells (the Rh factor is a marker). If you don't have it and it gets introduced into your body via your Rh positive baby, your body will try to gobble it up, wreaking havoc on the baby's blood cells.

The thing is, only sometimes during pregnancy (usually with trauma, some testing procedures, or delivery) does the baby's blood (and, consequently, Rh factor) get introduced into the mother's blood stream. It doesn't always happen. In fact, treatment for this potential problem didn't even exist until the late 1960s. But nowadays a rhogam shot is given as a precaution. Rhogam basically re-instructs your body not to attack the Rh factor.

Test: Complete blood count (CBC)

Tells: If you're anemic

Fearless Fact: True anemia is far more uncommon than most of us think. If you have it, though, and it's related to an iron or vitamin deficiency, you'll be treated with a supplement and some advice to eat iron-rich foods. You may also be advised to have further testing, because there are many types of anemia.

Test: Rubella immunity (also known as German measles)

Tells: If you're immune to rubella/German measles

Fearless Fact: Rubella, thankfully, is extremely rare. Most of us have been immunized, so chances are good that you, like the rest of us, are

Fake Anemia

Anemia, in general, is a condition in which there aren't enough healthy red blood cells to carry adequate oxygen to your tissues. But every pregnant woman gets dilutional (or what is sometimes called "fake") anemia. As a natural part of pregnancy, your blood volume (the liquid part) goes up significantly, but your blood cells won't increase at the same rate. Fake anemia develops as your blood naturally gets more diluted. This, along with weight gain, is a major reason why fatigue is so common in pregnancy.

Remember, dilutional anemia is a normal part of pregnancy. If your CBC shows your anemia is more severe, though, that's when your practitioner will recommend iron supplements or more testing. And don't be concerned about the supplements. They won't harm the baby, and there are even iron supplements that don't cause constipation.

immune. If you know you haven't been immunized, your chances of contracting it are still slim because, again, the rest of us have been. In the worst-case scenario (you're not immune and you're regularly around people who haven't been vaccinated), you will simply be told to stay away from speckled kids with fevers. Once you're pregnant, this is all you can do about not being immune.

Rubella Tip for Unvaccinated Women Who Plan Ahead

If you are merely contemplating getting pregnant and know you haven't been immunized for rubella previously—especially if you work with children or around people who are not usually vaccinated—we recommend getting tested before you try to conceive. If you indeed aren't immune, you can get the vaccine, wait a month, and then try to get pregnant.

Test: Thyroid testing

Tells: If your thyroid is under- or over-active

Fearless Fact: Thyroid disorders are easily controlled with medications, and all problems will be prevented before they ever start.

Thyroid Problems

Hypothyroidism is a condition in which your thyroid gland fails to make or release enough thyroid hormone. The result is a mix of symptoms, such as sluggishness, chronically cold hands and feet, constipation, dry skin, and a hoarse voice.

Hyperthyroidism is a condition in which your thyroid produces excessive amounts of hormone. Too much hormone can cause fatigue, muscle weakness, weight loss, increased heart rate, nervousness, irritability, and diarrhea.

Whether you're hypo or hyper, the condition can be controlled with medication if it's detected. It won't affect your pregnancy.

Test: Hepatitis B and C, syphilis, and HIV

Tells: If you have any of these sexually transmitted diseases (STDs).

Fearless Fact: Usually, babies do just fine when STDs are discovered early in the pregnancy and treatment is started promptly. Bear in mind that if any of these tests come back positive, the first step is to repeat the test or do further testing to find out if your results are accurate.

THE VAGINAL EXAM

Test: Pap test and vaginal cultures

Tells: If your cervical cells indicate pre-cancerous changes or if vaginal cultures indicate gonorrhea or chlamydia

Fearless Fact: Pre-cancerous changes in pregnancy are followed with observation. If treatment is ultimately required, it'll be initiated six weeks postpartum. This isn't something to be worried about. It takes a long time—years—for pre-cancerous cells to evolve into something more serious.

Gonorrhea and chlamydia are treatable with antibiotics. They shouldn't affect your pregnancy or baby.

Test: Urine culture

Tells: If infection is present.

Fearless Fact: Urinary tract infections (UTIs) are easily treated with antibiotics.

No Symptoms?

Having no symptoms of disorders such as STDs and urinary tract infections doesn't mean there are no problems. We call this being "asymptomatic." That means you don't feel it, but you still have it—and you need to be treated.

Women with some STDs, for example, can be asymptomatic for years. Left untreated, their condition can cause infection in their babies and possibly pneumonia or blindness. Asymptomatic urinary tract infections left untreated can invade the kidneys and lead to hospitalization or pre-term labor.

Fortunately, there's medicine to treat these problems, and none of it should affect your pregnancy or developing fetus. Just take the medicine even if you don't feel "sick."

Routine Testing: Round Two

(usually between twenty-four and twenty-eight weeks)

Test: One-hour post-glucola (diabetes) check

Tells: If you're developing pregnancy-related diabetes

Fearless Fact: If this test is abnormal, it doesn't mean you have diabetes just yet. It means you get what some lovingly call the three-hour torture test.

Illicit Drug Checks

If you have a history of drug use or are currently a drug user, you may also be asked to submit urine for occasional drug screens.

See also chapter 6, Fearless (Pregnant) Living.

THE DIABETES TEST

The one-hour post glucola test is the first step in screening for diabetes. If you don't pass this, you move on to the three-hour "torture" test—torture in the same way that standing in line at the DMV is torturous.

With your initial diabetes check (at around twenty-six to twenty-eight weeks), you'll be instructed to drink a bottle of sugary soda containing fifty grams (200 calories) of glucose or sugar, and then one hour later your blood will be drawn. (By the way, if you get the orange flavor, it tastes like super-sweet orange soda—not too bad if you drink it chilled.)

If you test positive, you will have to move on to the three-hour test. The three-hour test is when you have your blood drawn in a fasting state, and then you drink 100 grams of glucose and have your blood drawn every hour for three hours. You are not allowed to eat anything or drink anything but water during the three-hour process. Remember, though, that often when the one-hour is abnormal, the three-hour will come out normal, and you won't be labeled diabetic.

BLOOD TESTS

Test: CBC (again)

Tells: If you have anemia

Fearless Fact: Anemia is generally easily treated. See Round One.

Test: Antibody screen (for Rh-negative women only)

Tells: If you've developed antibodies to red blood cells

Fearless Fact: This is rare, and only certain antibodies cause problems in pregnancy. If this is the case, you'll likely be referred to a specialist. See Round One.

What's GBS?

GBS comes from your gastrointestinal tract, and about 10 to 20 percent of women are carriers. Once you have it in your system, you are known as a carrier, and the bacteria can essentially come and go whenever it feels inclined. GBS sometimes, but rarely, causes postpartum infection in the mom. The biggest concern is that the baby will contract the infection during the delivery process.

The female anatomy makes it easy for bacteria to spread from the rectal to the vaginal area. If the baby gets infected with GBS, it can become quite sick, necessitating an intensive care admission, intravenous fluids, antibiotics, spinal taps, chest x-rays, etc. To prevent this from happening, the Centers for Disease Control and Prevention recommend treating the mom in labor with intravenous antibiotics. Once you get the antibiotics, there's almost no chance that GBS will have any effect on your baby or you.

Routine Testing: Round Three

(usually between thirty-five and thirty-seven weeks)

THE VAGINAL CULTURE

Test: Group B Strep (GBS)

Tells: If you're a GBS carrier (see What's GBS?)

Fearless Fact: Only 10 to 20 percent of women are GBS carriers, but even if you are a carrier, you'll merely receive antibiotics while in labor. That's it.

From the Fearless Doc:
Genetic Testing

Test: First trimester prenatal screening (between eleven and fourteen weeks from the last menstrual period)

Tells: If blood levels and ultrasound indicate the baby *may* be affected by Down syndrome or a form of mental retardation

Fearless Fact: Even if you test positive, it *does not* mean your baby is abnormal. An amniocentesis will likely be recommended to verify.

Test: Chorionic villus sampling (between ten and twelve weeks from the last menstrual period)

Tells: If the baby has Down syndrome (also to detect a variety of other genetic disorders if indicated)

Fearless Fact: It's performed by a highly trained specialist called a perinatologist, and the risk of miscarriage is low (one in three hundred). Perk: Results come back fast, usually within three days.

Test: AFP/triple marker (between fifteen and twenty weeks from the last period)

Tells: If blood levels indicate the baby may be affected by neural tube defects. In most regions, this test is also still used to screen for increased risk of Down syndrome.

Fearless Fact: This test is known for a higher level of false positives, so don't be alarmed if your test comes back positive. If it does, you'll likely be referred for an amniocentesis.

Test: Quadruple marker prenatal screen

Tells: If blood levels indicate an increased risk of Down syndrome, Trisomy 18 and neural tube or abdominal wall defects.

Fearless Fact: Although there are far fewer false positives, they still exist. So don't panic if your test comes back positive. If it does, you'll likely be referred for an amniocentesis.

Test: Amniocentesis (usually between fourteen and sixteen weeks from the last period)

Tells: If the baby has Down syndrome or other chromosomal abnormalities

Fearless Fact: The anxiety leading up to this test is far worse than the test itself. The risk of miscarriage is extremely low (one in five hundred), but results take seven to twenty-one days to come back.

Test: Genetic ultrasound (between eighteen and twenty weeks from the last period)

Tells: If the baby has major anatomic defects, including spina bifida, and if the mother's uterus, ovaries, etc., appear normal

Fearless Fact: It's painless and actually fun to see the baby. This is also your opportunity to learn the gender, if you choose.

Fast and Fearless

Here's all you need to know about prenatal testing:

- The overwhelming majority of babies are born without defects.
- It's almost automatic to have three rounds of routine testing (blood, Pap, cultures, etc.) and a few ultrasounds, but further genetic testing is highly optional.
- If anything is discovered with the routine testing, it's usually easily treated without risk to the baby.
- Consider asking for the first trimester prenatal screen. If it's available in your area, it may negate your need/desire for any further genetic testing (that is, CVS or amniocentesis).

- Just because you're over thirty-five doesn't mean you have to get a CVS or an amniocentesis. Your own health, your genetic family history, and the results you get from the first trimester prenatal screen and/or AFP/triple marker are also important factors to consider.
- If you decide to get an amniocentesis, know that the fear factor has been extremely overblown. It reportedly is not painful, and it only lasts twenty seconds!
- If you get an amniocentesis or CVS, you may experience light cramping and spotting. Go home and put your feet up.
- Understand that genetic testing checks only for chromosomal abnormality (certain forms of mental retardation and Down syndrome, typically). No test can check that each and every gene is "perfect" (assuming we even knew or agreed on what "perfect" is).

4

Fearless Diet, Weight Gain, and Exercise

"People don't understand that for me it is much more than just gaining/losing weight. It is about losing my single, independent, young, non-mom image. While men become sexy dads, women become matronly. I'm sure men see you completely differently. I'll never have 'it' again."

– from the pregnancy journal of Sarah, mother of six-month-old Ash

*"I worried about my weight gain; however,
I accepted that gaining weight at a healthy rate
was important to the health of my baby.
I tried to eat healthy, even though I didn't exercise as
much as I would have liked during my pregnancy
because I was spending a lot of long hours at work.
I ended up gaining about thirty pounds during my pregnancy,
most of it in the second and third trimesters.
I've been very lucky; I lost about twenty-six pounds
within six weeks of the birth of my son.
Now it's a matter of losing the rest!"*

– Dorothy, mother of six-month-old Edison

FEAR: I'm going to gain so much weight!

FEARLESS FACT: It's temporary!

To sane, nonpregnant people, this fear may sound ridiculous. Of course you're going to gain weight! You will likely weigh more than you've ever weighed in your life. Thankfully, though, you have an excellent excuse: You're pregnant, remember? Now let's talk about this murkier area of pregnancy weight gain. How much is too much?

Despite girl power, many of us—far too many—like to see certain magic numbers on the doc's Detecto scale. I wish we didn't even have to be weighed! Incidentally, in many more civilized parts of the world, pregnant women aren't routinely weighed. This info comes from my friend Hadley, who had one child in California and then moved to New Zealand and had her second child there. She never once got weighed during her second pregnancy, and she said it was heavenly. But, of course, our medical establishment claims we must be weighed to ensure we're gaining properly.

Know that you're going to likely gain between twenty-five and forty-five pounds, although some women gain more and are perfectly healthy. Know that there's a list of things that account for this weight gain: the amniotic fluid, uterine enlargement, placenta, maternal breast tissue, fluids in the tissue, maternal blood volume, the baby (!), and, oh yes, maternal fat. Your doctor or midwife will tell you whether you're gaining too much. Otherwise, just eat sensibly and realize the weight will start coming off once you deliver. I've had friends who've gained fifty or sixty pounds during pregnancy, and I've had friends who've gained twenty-five pounds. By their children's first birthdays, it's impossible to guess who gained a lot and who gained a little. It really can come off.

Your Weight Gain Is Genetically Predetermined (Mostly)

FEARLESS DOC

We can't discuss diet and nutrition without encountering that universal fear in pregnancy: weight gain! Let's put this one to rest right now. *As long as you practice some moderation and self-control, the amount of weight you gain is pretty much genetically predetermined.* Some women can pay no attention to their diet and gain only twenty-five pounds during their pregnancies, and others who focus way too much attention and care on their diet might gain sixty pounds. This is another one of those things you can blame on your parents.

The average weight gain in pregnancy is a meaningless number that causes much anguish for those who exceed it. The only person you can compare yourself to is you in your previous pregnancies. If this is your first pregnancy, then all you can do is eat prudently and trust your practitioner to reassure you that what you gain appears normal for you. If your doctor or midwife thinks you're gaining too much or too little, he or she will make suggestions.

If this is your second pregnancy, you can expect to gain about the same amount as your first. Remember, though, that your final weight may be more or less, depending on where you started. So weight gain is one of those things that you can't control beyond complying with a healthy diet and exercise program. Knowing this may make you feel a little better about the inevitable changes your body is making for the sake of the little one inside of you.

The Weight Gain "Formula"

FEARLESS Midwife

Aaaahhhhhh, weight gain! For some people, their whole pregnancy seems to revolve around their weight gain. How can it not? Unless you've belonged to Weight Watchers in the past, when have you ever had to routinely be weighed in front of other people?

Weighing in is usually one of the first things you do at every appointment, and then you sit in trepidation waiting for a nod of approval or condemnation. Let me set you straight on a few things about weight gain. The amount of weight you officially should gain is calculated by your existing height and weight. The formula goes something like this:

- If you are underweight for your height, you get to gain thirty-five to forty-five pounds.

- Average weight earns you twenty-five to thirty-five extra pounds.
- If you're overweight, try to stick to fifteen to twenty-five pounds.

Having said that, the truth is, every woman seems to gain around forty pounds no matter where she starts. Well, all right, maybe not every woman, but forty is a more realistic number. The only women who actually manage to keep their weight gain at twenty-five pounds seem to be naturally skinny or extremely body conscious. The rest of us get to forty pounds quite easily. And others manage to put on even more weight, sometimes topping out at sixty to one hundred pounds.

See also Too Much or Too Little?, *on page 82.*

Don't Let Fear Dictate Your Diet

FEARLESS DOC

You may be inundated with articles, advertisements, and hearsay from well-meaning friends telling you what to eat and drink and what to avoid. The message seems to be, if you don't/do eat/drink X, Y, and Z, the body that you have always known is going to suddenly fall apart and fail you just because you're pregnant. So what *should* you eat and drink?

The quick answer is anything. In your nonpregnant life, you probably already knew that fruits and vegetables, lean meats, nuts, vegetable oils, and grains were good for you and that loads of sugar and saturated fat weren't so healthy. You probably also knew that gallons of caffeine and excessive amounts of alcohol weren't good. The same holds true in pregnancy. Please remember that your body is very wise. You must have been healthy and, therefore, eating a healthy enough diet just to ovulate and conceive. Your body knows what to do. We aren't so fragile a species that a healthy fetus would succumb to a few Twinkies, a rare glass of wine, or a missed vitamin tablet.

MORE ON DRINKS

It flies in the face of everything pregnant moms are told these days, but the truth is moderate amounts of caffeine—the equivalent of two cups of coffee, for example—are fine. What about the occasional glass of wine or a sip of your husband's beer? That's harmless too. Of course, my "occasional" may be different from yours. Let me define it more clearly: a glass of wine a week (in a average-size wine glass). If you're drinking more and/or can't seem to control your need to drink alcohol while you're pregnant, you have a problem; seek help pronto.

And on Herbal Teas

When it comes to herbs, there's not a lot of evidence to say what's safe in pregnancy and what's not. Most of the stuff you buy at the grocery store—raspberry and chamomile teas, for example—appears to be perfectly safe.

See also Chapter 6, Fearless (Pregnant) Living.

FEAR: I won't be able to control those pregnancy cravings.

FEARLESS FACT: Cravings shouldn't always be controlled.

Cravings in pregnancy are pretty normal. Come to think of it, cravings in nonpregnant life are fairly normal too. One line of thought, although it hasn't been scientifically proved, is that a craving is telling you to eat something you may be missing in your diet. I swear I had cravings for more vegetables, avocados, and olive oil in my pregnancy. But I also liked milkshakes and didn't pass up too many french fries. Some of my friends craved cheese, chocolate milk, pineapple, cheeseburgers, cereal, or apples. You're just as likely to crave "good" foods as you are to crave "bad" ones.

Some studies have linked pregnancy cravings with hormonal fluxes. That's why, they say, cravings typically dissipate after the first trimester (although most women I know say their cravings came and went through most of the pregnancy). Cravings do seem to dissipate, however, very late in pregnancy. What I say is that it's because you've eaten through everything by that time and you're ready to have the kid and get a little leaner, although I'm not sure any scientist would support this hypothesis. Here's my tip: Indulge your cravings, but don't overindulge (you don't need two McDonald's shakes in one day; one will do just fine). Then move on.

SWEET TOOTH?

If you crave sweets, eat them during the day. At bedtime, try a snack that's protein-based. You'll avoid possible low blood sugar, which will help you sleep better and, possibly, avoid weird dreams, sweats, and headaches. Try a few spoonfuls of peanut butter, a hard-boiled egg, or a piece of chicken or turkey.

How Often You Eat Is Important

FEARLESS DOC

Much more important than what you eat is how often you eat each day. In your busy, nonpregnant life, you may eat only a couple of times a day, going hours between meals and avoiding snacks for vanity's sake. This isn't a healthy pattern and is absolutely to be avoided when pregnant.

Once you know you're pregnant, you need to begin to eat about six or seven times a day. Try small amounts every two to three hours and, overall, attempt to eat from the various food groups. This will keep your blood sugar in a more constant range, which is healthy for your baby. Your body is like a steam engine on a train. When you put a log on the fire every few hours, the engine burns steadily. When you throw all the logs on the fire at once, the engine burns very hot and then grows cold. You will go farther with fewer maintenance problems if you eat small amounts frequently.

Too Much or Too Little?

FEARLESS Midwife

If you gain too little weight, we know that your baby is more likely to be too little. Sometimes these babies are growth restricted because they aren't getting enough nourishment, or perhaps they are just tiny and don't have a lot of strength to eat after they're born.

If you gain too much when you're pregnant, you're more likely to have complications with high blood pressure, diabetes, or a baby that gets extremely big and just won't fit! If nothing else, you will be just plain miserable. If you weren't pregnant and gained sixty pounds, you wouldn't be happy. Excessive weight gain combined with pregnancy will cause swelling, back pain, and low energy. You may not think that's a big deal, but when your ankles are as big as your thighs, trust me, you will be miserable!

The solution is to eat sensibly. You need only an average of about 300 calories extra a day. That's not so much—just about the number of calories in a container of fruited yogurt and an eight-ounce glass of orange juice.

FEAR: My mother is overweight and always blamed it on having kids. I'm terrified this will happen to me.

FEARLESS FACT: It's usually not just the kids; it's the kids, plus the Cheetos.

This was definitely one of my fears. I grew up hearing about how thin my mother was until she had children. I even led a tortured childhood having to sit through Weight Watchers meetings with her. (All I can remember about them is you get in big trouble if you, say, accidentally kick over a can of TAB in the meeting room.)

Here's the deal with weight and pregnancy. After about six months postpartum, most women are back to their pre-pregnancy weight, plus a few pounds (from two to ten). There are some caveats to this. I'll start with the optimistic one first.

Several women I know have actually ended up thinner after having children. This happened to my friend Kim, for instance, who says she just stopped being able to focus so much attention on food. Instead, she had to care for her two sons. My sister-in-law JoAnna was the thinnest she's ever been after her third child. She attributes this to breast-feeding, which burns an extra 500 or so calories a day.

Even when you're caring for a baby and breast-feeding, however, my personal experience is that it doesn't take much time to pop 500 calories of chocolate-covered raisins in your mouth (for my mother it was Cheetos). When you get good at breast-feeding, you can even do it while you eat. That means most of us don't end up thinner or even as thin, but the fallout isn't as bad as you might imagine, either—just a few extra pounds.

Now for the second and less pleasant caveat: a few extra pounds here and there tend to really build up over the years. Say you're eight pounds heavier a year after the baby, and then, voila, you get pregnant with number two! Guess what? After the second, you're another eight pounds heavier. So here you are, sixteen pounds from your pre-motherhood weight. Maybe that's how having children takes the rap for women getting fat. But, then again, perhaps we'd all be chubby even if we didn't have kids.

Feel free to make your own unscientific observations, as I did, on this matter. Look at all the women you know, break them down into age groups, and then compare them. Do the ones who don't have children have flawless figures compared with the ones who do? Okay, I'll just give you the answer: nope. I have friends who have children, and I have friends who don't; and as far as I can tell, the ones without are no better off figure-wise than the ones with.

What Shouldn't You Eat?

FEARLESS DOC

No pregnancy is immune to rumors and hearsay about what is safe to eat and what foods are considered taboo. The Food and Drug Administration does a pretty good job regulating the sanitation and quality of the food we buy in the United States. For this reason, you can pretty much eat anything you desire as long as it's in moderation.

Salmon or halibut for dinner once a week, sushi at a reputable restaurant, or even an occasional glass of wine won't harm your baby. It's unlikely you'll get "mad cow" disease from eating a hamburger or a good steak! You might get an upset stomach if you eat something that disagrees with you, but that's a chance we all take when we put food in our mouths. And most women's bodies aren't so fragile that getting sick will harm a little baby tucked safely away in its mother's womb.

Five Easy Tips for Good Pregnancy Nutrition

FEARLESS Midwife

Some women can rattle off the calorie, carb, and protein counts of almost anything on the supermarket shelves. Others, well..., let's just say pregnancy is the first time you've truly been concerned about anything other than taste. Rest assured, though, that there's no need to hire a nutritionist or otherwise become fixated on every morsel that goes into your mouth. For sound nutrition during pregnancy, focus on these five tips:

1. **Water:** Drink eight to ten glasses a day. The human body is composed mainly of water. The baby is a human floating in a bag of water. Besides,

you need water to maintain your increasing blood volume and fluid levels. Drink up.

2. **Calcium:** You need 1,200 to 1,500 milligrams a day. If you don't get it in your diet, then supplement. A prenatal vitamin will give you 200 to 250 milligrams; that's the equivalent of one serving, and you need about five servings total per day.
3. **Iron:** You need sixty milligrams of elemental iron a day. If you're taking a prenatal supplement, you're covered. If not, take a separate iron supplement.
4. **Protein:** You need sixty to one hundred grams a day. Practically everything has some protein in it. If you eat meat or dairy, you will not have a problem at all. As an example, four ounces of meat contain twenty-five grams. One glass of milk has ten grams. If you're a vegetarian, you know that beans, nuts, and tofu are good sources. A half-cup of soybeans or a half-cup of peanuts has about ten grams of protein.
5. **Fruits and vegetables:** If you focus on your calcium, iron, and protein, you'll be pretty well stuffed for the day. Just fill in the blanks with lots of fruits and vegetables.

Examples of Nutrient-Rich Food Choices...

- **Calcium-rich foods:** yogurt, milk, cheese, spinach, fortified cereals, and fortified orange juice
- **Iron-rich foods:** lean red meats, chicken, turkey, beans, fortified cereals, and blackstrap molasses
- **Protein-rich foods:** eggs, chicken, and other meats, as well as peanut butter, hummus, and tofu

Don't Diet

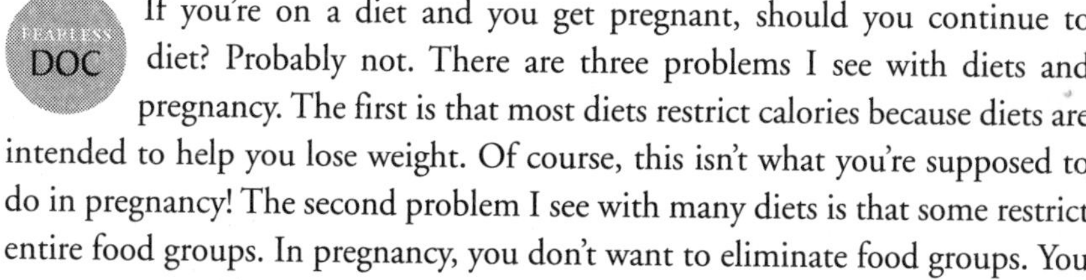

If you're on a diet and you get pregnant, should you continue to diet? Probably not. There are three problems I see with diets and pregnancy. The first is that most diets restrict calories because diets are intended to help you lose weight. Of course, this isn't what you're supposed to do in pregnancy! The second problem I see with many diets is that some restrict entire food groups. In pregnancy, you don't want to eliminate food groups. You want to eat a wide variety of foods.

Of course, if your "diet" merely forbids sugar and other empty carbs but doesn't restrict your calories for weight loss, and if it's filled with vegetables, fruits, whole grains, lean meats, healthy fats, and low-fat dairy products, by all means stay on it.

The third issue I have with diets and pregnancy, however, is the most important: I don't want any pregnant woman to obsess about what she eats. Diets tend to cause you to count grams, calories, or whatever. It's fear-based living, promoting the idea that if you don't get X amount of this or that nutrient, you'll somehow suffer the consequences. This simply isn't necessary for a healthy pregnancy.

FEAR: My husband will not like how pregnancy affects my body.

FEARLESS FACT: He'll be too in awe of you and then too busy with fatherhood to notice.

If your husband is a real fitness fanatic—or, more to the point, he likes you to be one—he and you may be worried about your body or about whether he'll find you attractive after the baby is born. I'll start with a disclaimer: This is his baby too, and he should be more attracted to you, not less, because you've incubated the little being. Okay, now for some reality.

My friend S. (who shall remain nameless lest her husband file for divorce) told me that pre-fatherhood, her husband had always been one to make jokes about women's weight. Perhaps you have one of these guys too, the ones who snicker and make snide comments when they see a portly woman pushing a stroller. Maybe he says, "I sure hope that doesn't happen to your butt when we have kids! Ha-ha-ha." What he doesn't realize is that you too would prefer that your derriere remain unchanged, but you're not willing to laugh at anyone else and tempt fate.

S. said that most of the fear she and her husband had about weight came in the first trimester, before she'd even gained any. This is quite common. The anticipation of "losing your figure" is bad, but once you get into really being pregnant, that fear gets crossed off the list really fast. With S., her husband's backpedaling strategy was to tell her that she shouldn't worry because she'd certainly lose the weight and never be like those women he joked about. This "encouragement" actually made things worse!

S. started to feel an enormous amount of pressure. Barely into her first trimester, she was already worrying that she wouldn't lose the pregnancy weight quickly and that her husband would judge her negatively for it. S. tried to counter by informing her husband it would take a long, long time for her to lose the weight; she wanted to lessen his expectation. Guess what? She and her husband got into a huge fight because he accused her of resolving to have a mediocre body after the pregnancy.

What's the lesson from all this? Let's check in with S. now: "The irony of this whole fear is that we've been so consumed with the baby in the first six months that weight is hardly discussed, and when it is, my husband has been entirely complimentary."

This is how it goes. By the time you have the baby, your husband will have grown up considerably. In the meantime, let him know that his comments and concerns about weight are like powder kegs when pregnancy hormones are circulating through your body. If they're shared with you—KA-BOOM!—a fight, or at the least hurt feelings, will transpire. Of course, he has a right and perhaps a need to voice his fears and concerns. Advise him to start a support group with his male friends or seek therapy for being a jerk.

Sympathy Weight

If you're worried that your husband isn't going to take well to your expanded girth and/or the aftermath, keep your fingers crossed that a phenomenon called "sympathy weight" hits him. Some men have been known to pack on forty pounds right along with their pregnant wives!

FEAR: I've lost a lot of weight with diet and exercise. Now I'm scared I'm going to gain it all back.

FEARLESS FACT: You'll be far better off for having lost the weight.

It takes some serious vanity control to lose a lot of weight and then get pregnant! But here's the thing, you will be far better off afterward for having lost the weight beforehand. My friend Jennifer went on Weight Watchers, lost thirty pounds, and then gained approximately fifty pounds during her pregnancy. She had a healthy baby girl, and by six months postpartum she'd lost all the weight except ten pounds. That means that after having a baby, she was still twenty pounds lighter than her pre–Weight Watchers days.

She says there are some serious perks, not drawbacks, to having lost weight previously. When she was pregnant, she didn't feel the panic that many women feel over gaining weight. Instead, she felt she had a plan in place. Once she had the baby and was through with breast-feeding, she knew she could resume her Weight Watchers program and lose weight. She was already successful at it. She also said that, unlike most women, the weigh-ins at each doctor visit didn't bother her. She was used to them.

On Vitamin Supplements

FEARLESS DOC

A daily vitamin supplement is recommended in pregnancy, but is it imperative? Not exactly. I think of it more like insurance. The truth is that even if you don't regularly take vitamins before or even during your pregnancy, your baby will still be born healthy in this country. Why? Because the American diet is incredibly rich compared to most places on Earth.

Special Concerns: Eating Disorders

Women who've battled eating disorders such as anorexia or bulimia may require special dietary guidelines, need to be monitored more closely, and/or need counseling or a support group. Binging/purging, taking laxatives to lose weight, or not eating are totally unacceptable in pregnancy. If you don't have your disease under control, this is something you should be fearful about. You need to discuss this with your doctor or midwife, and you need to get help. Once you get the disorder under control, you have the same odds of delivering a healthy baby as anyone else.

In fact, many of our foods—breads, cereal, milk, and orange juice, for example—are often fortified with additional vitamins. Eating these foods and all the wonderful produce available in our markets ensures your growing baby will not suffer from vitamin deficiencies. Your baby will take from your excesses all that it needs to grow.

The real benefit to taking a prenatal vitamin, however, is that it contains a specific nutrient that's highly effective at preventing neural tube defects such as spina bifida and anencephaly: folate (or folic acid). I encourage women to take folic acid as soon they know they're pregnant or begin trying to conceive.

You can also get folic acid by eating green leafy vegetables and bread and grains, which are now fortified with it. The recommended dose is 800 to 1,000 micrograms per day. While you can get your folate in a prenatal multivitamin, some women, I've found, can't stomach the vitamin, especially in the first trimester. If this is you, know that you can stop taking prenatal multivitamins and take only a folate supplement until your morning sickness ceases. Then, if you like, you can resume your prenatal vitamin.

FEAR: The skin on my stomach won't be able to accommodate the gain.

FEARLESS FACT: Elastin and collagen ensure that skin stretches just fine.

It doesn't seem possible at the outset of pregnancy, but your skin really will stretch enough to accommodate the baby. Collagen and elastin in the skin guarantee it. I'm told collagen has the tensile strength of steel (by the end of the pregnancy, you'll understand why this is important). Elastin, just like the name implies, comprises the rubber-like, elastic fibers in the skin. From the scientific perspective, each elastin molecule will uncoil into a more extended conformation when the fiber is stretched and will recoil spontaneously as soon as the stretching force is relaxed. In English: You pretty much bounce back when the babe is born. However, there may be a couple of telltale signs.

Stretch Marks!

It's a universal fear of every newly pregnant woman: stretch marks. And the question looms, will I or won't I get them? Statistics are against you (some say as many as 90 percent of women get them on their abdomen, breasts, and/or thighs), but here's why you shouldn't fear them:

- The tendency toward stretch marks is inherited, and you certainly can't change your genetics.
- You've done your best to gain weight gradually; there's not much more you can do.
- You've slathered your body with moisturizers. But you won't want to waste too much money on special stretch-mark creams. No topical treatment has been proven to prevent them.

- Even if you get stretch marks, they do fade somewhat over time.
- You probably don't dress like Beyoncé very often anyhow.
- There's always laser treatment if the marks are really bad. (Consult your dermatologist four to six months after the pregnancy.)

Fat Ankles

FEARLESS Midwife

Eating melon, sleeping on the left side, swimming…these are some of the tricks that women say work to keep ankles from swelling. Feet, ankles, and legs swell because of the weight of your uterus; it compresses your pelvic veins and creates poor circulation. When the blood isn't able to flow back as it normally would, it pools in your lower extremities and creates swelling because of gravity. It's not attractive, and it might require you to ditch your usual stilettos and don bedroom slippers, but know that it's completely normal and harmless *unless* your blood pressure is also rising. The only thing that really seems to work, by the way, is lying on your side with your feet raised. I actually had one patient who "lost" fifteen pounds (it was water weight) in one weekend by staying on the couch.

FEAR: People will think I'm fat, not pregnant.

FEARLESS FACT: No they won't, because you'll just tell them, "I'm pregnant!"

Okay, we've all heard the horror stories of someone asking a woman, "When are you due?" only to find out she's portly and/or wearing an A-line dress or some other maternity-like fashion. (Women of child-bearing age with an extra thirty pounds to lose, of course, should take care not to wear these things.) But truthfully, this horror story rarely happens in the reverse. I've never heard of anyone assuming a pregnant woman is just fat, even though all pregnant women seem to fear this. Precisely because of the above-mentioned horror story, few people will say anything unless you first tell them you're pregnant. Men, especially, will not say anything, which will lead you to believe that every male thinks you're fat.

I saw my pal Kathryn handle this well. She was eight months pregnant and ran into an old acquaintance, who happened to be male. She had a complete conversation with him while we stood there. He kept his eyes on her face and seemed intent on not letting them stray. Finally, with a perfectly straight face, he asked her, "So what's new with you?" She blurted, "Well..., I'm pregnant!" She should've said, "Well, I'm pregnant, moron," but she was too kind.

The moral of this is, make it a practice to blurt out that you're pregnant whenever you have the chance and as soon as possible. It'll make people more comfortable recognizing it, and it'll ease your mind that no one will misperceive that you are weighty without a good reason.

Veiny Issues

Even a normal amount of pregnancy weight gain, however, can have some unpleasant side effects: purplish, superficial veins called spider veins, bulging and painful veins called varicose veins, and hemorrhoids, which are basically varicose veins of the anus (isn't that interesting?). This is due to increased pressure from the uterus on the pelvic veins, which increases pressure on the leg veins. Hormone-induced relaxation of the muscle tissue in the veins also contributes.

All of these problems are typical in pregnancy, although you should point them out to your doctor or midwife. He or she will definitely recommend balancing periods of rest (in the horizontal position) with exercise, which promotes healthy circulation. Also, avoid straining when going to the bathroom. Drink lots of water and eat fiber-rich foods to make it easier; using an over-the-counter stool softener occasionally is also fine. Other tips include wearing maternity support hose, available through a maternity store or your OB/GYN, and spending as much time as possible in baths and swimming pools (which takes off some of the pressure caused by gravity).

Getting Fat Down There

It isn't common with first pregnancies, but in subsequent pregnancies you may also see varicose veins in your vulva (say that three times fast). What you'll notice is a swollen labia, and you may think something is definitely wrong down there.

Again, the culprit is the pressure of the uterus pushing on your pelvic veins. It'll go away once you have the baby. In the meantime, ask your practitioner about perineal support garments, and also follow the recommendations for varicose veins.

Postpartum Weight

With the birth of your baby, you'll lose an average of fifteen to twenty pounds. Whatever you've gained beyond that is what you have left to deal with. What I usually see is that most women are about ten pounds from their pre-pregnancy weight at their six-week visit. Maybe 5 percent of the women I see, though, aren't anywhere near it. Bear in mind that it took you nine months to gain the weight, and it might take that long to lose it. Don't be too hard on yourself. Even if you weren't postpartum, it would take you several months to lose twenty-five or so pounds!

There's good news for women who breast-feed: it burns up about 500 calories a day (although mothers who breast-feed also tend to be hungrier and

Your Midsection Immediately After the Birth

If you had a bikini body before pregnancy, you will be appalled. You'll likely think you'll never again wear anything less than a parka. Elizabeth, a woman I met at a baby shower, told me the first thing she thought was how sorry she felt for her husband. The first thing I thought was how sorry I felt for me!

Try not to panic. Swollen, jiggly, and, well, jelly-belly-ish is how almost everyone looks. Thankfully, things improve drastically by the time you're one month postpartum. A lot of the swelling goes down, and your skin begins the bounce-back process (although "bounce" might not be the right word; it's a little slower than that). By six months postpartum, you may look just as good as you did before you got pregnant. You could still be a tad squishy in the middle, but you definitely won't look all that unusual.

may eat more). And I can guarantee that all new mothers are so busy with the newborn they don't have a lot of time to fuss over food, which might work to your weight advantage. By your baby's first birthday, you'll likely be pleasantly surprised to see how much weight you've lost without trying all that hard.

~ *Fast and Fearless*

Here's all you need to know about food and pregnancy:

- Try to eat a variety of foods and focus on getting water, iron, calcium, and protein.
- Eat frequently. Six small meals a day are better than three huge ones.
- Fruits, vegetables, and lean meats are always a good idea, pregnant or not.
- No foods are taboo, despite what you may hear. Moderation is key.
- A prenatal supplement isn't essential, but it will help with your iron and calcium. It also has folic acid, which is important.

FEAR: I'll have to stop exercising.

FEARLESS FACT: You may have to alter some activities, but exercise in pregnancy is usually encouraged.

After my friend Karen, who's a yoga instructor but also surfs and skis, found out she was pregnant, she had conflicting thoughts. "I just got a new surfboard; I'd better get out and use it while I can. No, wait a minute, I'd better not do anything."

What's the reality? You can pretty much do any exercise as long as you don't get dizzy, overheated, or dehydrated and as long as you won't suffer blows to the abdomen or hard falls. Truthfully, you probably shouldn't surf or ski. (If you're a pro surfer or skier, the likelihood that you'll wipe out may be slim, but this is general advice for the rest of us.)

Some pregnant women, however, aren't comfortable exercising without more support and guidance. I've known women who've joined pregnancy gyms, taken prenatal exercise classes (yoga, of course, is extremely popular), and even hired trainers during their pregnancy. If you have the money for a trainer, I say save it for after the pregnancy. You're probably not going to feel like giving it your all once you get into the serious throes of pregnancy.

And speaking of serious throes of pregnancy, you'll probably also want to scale down a really serious exercise program. I was an avid exerciser before getting pregnant, and I exercised throughout my pregnancy, but by the last few weeks I wasn't doing much more than walking the dog and waiting for *shavasana* in a prenatal yoga class (that's the pose where you get to lie down).

See also Exercise Scale-down, *page 103.*

Exercise Pointers

Unless your practitioner gives you specific restrictions or instructions, you should keep active during pregnancy. This may be as simple as walking every day to get your heart rate moving, or it may be a full-blown fitness program designed to be safe during pregnancy.

Exercise and fitness are activities that you can control. They are important in pregnancy, just as they are during every other time of life. We all feel better when we're active, and this alone can make your pregnancy more enjoyable. Exercise will likely improve your mood and help you enjoy the weeks as they fly by. It also may help you be better prepared for the rigors of labor and improve your ability to reach inside of yourself when that little bit extra is called for. Here are some guidelines for safe exercise:

- **Keep your heart rate moderate.** Aim to keep your peak pulse rate below 140. Above this level, your body may begin to divert blood away from the uterus and your baby. This is probably not significant until the third trimester, but it's still a good rule to follow. You can get a heart rate monitor at any sporting goods store or just use this rule of thumb: You should be able to carry on a conversation while you exercise.
- **Stay hydrated.** Always drink lots of fluids when you work out. Dehydration can cause dizziness, a tendency to faint, a drop in blood pressure, increased heart rate, and pre-term contractions.
- **Don't strain your back.** Avoid any lifting using your lower back. Whether it's a twenty-pound weight or a paper clip, you should always lift with your knees instead of your back. This is important because your lower back is already taxed due to your growing midsection. Also, placental hormones cause relaxation of the ligaments, which is good for labor but makes it easier to pull or strain body parts.
- **Avoid jarring exercises.** This is most relevant in the later months, but step classes or jogging may have too much impact. Spin classes, fast walking, and supervised weight training are all safe in pregnancy. Possibly the best exercise for the pregnant woman is a swimming or pool training class since the strain on your ligaments and back is virtually eliminated.

Use Your Head When You Use Your Body

FEARLESS Midwife

Common sense is one of the best gauges as to what you can do while pregnant. Certainly, walking, swimming, jogging (in the first few months), light weightlifting, and yoga are all great for you and your baby. Jumping from an airplane, reckless off-road cycling, and karate kicks to the abdomen are a bit extreme and should be avoided.

I always tell women to listen to their bodies. If, during or after exercise, you feel crampy, have bleeding, have increased joint pain, or just don't feel well, your body is sending you a message. The key is to pay attention and act accordingly. Slow down, change what you're doing, or stop. Of course, the idea is not to put yourself in a position where you might experience trauma to your abdomen or overexert yourself. You'll have plenty of time for that after the baby is born. Just try picking up a toddler who's having a temper tantrum!

Know Your Postpartum Exercise Priorities

FEARLESS Midwife

Women often ask me how quickly they can get back to their exercise regimens after they have the baby. The official answer is about six weeks. My answer is always to take it easy, but *not* because postpartum exercise will cause problems.

I tell them to take it easy because they have their whole lives to spend exercising and getting back into shape, and they'll have time with their newborn only once. I want them to relax and enjoy their babies as much as possible. That's what they'll remember years from now, not the five-pound advantage they got from getting back to the gym a couple of months sooner.

The Other Exercises

FEARLESS DOC

Kegel exercises, a repetitive squeezing of the muscles of the vagina, improve tone and may help with your delivery and recovery. To know that you're doing this correctly, imagine that you are trying to stop the flow of urine in the middle of voiding. Try this squeezing and relaxing in sets of ten to twenty up to ten times a day. Tell your nonpregnant friends about this as well. You, and they, may notice increased enjoyment from intercourse as an added benefit of this exercise.

The Hidden Perk of the Gym: Inspiration

Going to the gym while you're pregnant can be incredibly encouraging. You'll probably be surprised at how supportive everyone is. I always felt great after a class because so many people would tell me how inspiring it was for them that I was exercising while I was pregnant.

When you're growing rapidly, this encouragement means a lot! The funny thing too was that most of them were a source of inspiration for me. Before I got pregnant, I looked around my gym and noticed how many of the women were in great shape, despite having a few children. It's good to know it's possible—and not just if you're Uma Thurman or Gwyneth Paltrow.

The Mommy Factor: Gyms with Childcare

My friend Angela sums up the exercise/kids dilemma well. "If I can somehow get my four-and almost-three-year-old out the door for a walk around the lake, I often feel like the planets must all be aligned!"

One idea is to check out gyms with childcare. The major chains and even some of the smaller gyms have childcare for a couple of bucks an hour. Sometimes you have to wait until your baby is six months old, but many gyms are also relaxing this age limit. You won't know until your baby gets there, of course, if his or her temperament will be a good match early on. But by six months, most babies will tolerate childcare at least long enough for you to do a half-hour on the treadmill. If you're lucky enough to have a compliant kid, perhaps you'll even manage a whole class.

In the final month, you may also want to begin to exercise your perineum. This is the area that lies between your vagina and anus, and it needs to stretch as the baby is delivered. You can help prepare your body for this by massaging this area gently. Place your thumb, or have your partner put two fingers, into your vagina and gently push toward your anus while moving slowly back and forth. Using a lubricant like K-Y Jelly is helpful. Also, moisturizing the outside skin of the perineum with vitamin E oil will help its elasticity. Note: Women with a history of herpes should avoid this since it may cause a breakout.

If You Plan to Breast-feed, Exercise Your Neck Now

A week after delivery, I was in the chiropractor's office with severe neck pain. The problem: breast-feeding. I was constantly looking down and struggling to get it right. The chiropractor told me that he saw many new moms for the very same reason. If I'd come to him prior to delivery, he said, he would have told me to prepare by doing neck exercises. The best thing to do is simple stretches as often as you want throughout the day. Here are two he recommended:

TENSION RELEASE

Sit up straight in a chair, tuck your chin slightly, and tilt your head to the left. Place your left hand on the upper right side of your head, gently pull to the left, and hold for sixty seconds. Repeat on the other side.

FACE CLOCK

Lie on your back with your knees bent and your feet flat on the floor. Look straight up. Imagine your head against the face of a clock. Slowly draw the outer edge of the clock with your nose. Go clockwise first, then counterclockwise. Repeat this two times in each direction.

FEAR: I'm going to over-stretch in yoga.

FEARLESS FACT: Yoga and other stretching classes can be modified.

As the pregnancy progresses, your risk of muscle strain or tearing may increase because the connective tissues in the body become more elastic than normal. This is why jumping or jarring motions or quick changes in direction aren't a great idea. It's also why some women say they become extremely flexible and fear over-stretching. I've taken yoga for years and didn't experience phenomenal gains in flexibility when I was pregnant, but I realize it's common.

What's the solution? You should always tell your yoga instructor (or any fitness instructor, for that matter) that you're pregnant. I was pleasantly surprised by how many instructors had children and could offer great modifications. If you're particularly concerned, try taking prenatal classes. They're a great way to experience some mom-to-be camaraderie, and they also help ensure

New Regimes Are Fine Too

What about the old adage, don't start any new exercise program when you're pregnant? That's no longer true. While pregnant women are still discouraged from doing extreme sports, most reasonable exercise programs are fine. Often, when women get pregnant, it's the first time in their lives that they've felt motivated to live a healthy lifestyle. Take advantage of the motivation and get moving!

that you're working with a qualified instructor. And here's the best protection: Never stretch until it hurts or force yourself into an uncomfortable position.

See also the Exercise Scale-down *chart on pages 104–105.*

The Famous Sit-up Question

FEARLESS Midwife

One of the most frequently asked questions I encounter is, can I do sit-ups? By all means, if you can do a sit-up, then do one! You'll know when you can't do them anymore, and there isn't any way the exercise is going to harm your baby. When the time comes that sit-ups are out, you can either skip the ab exercises or ask an instructor at the gym to show you some alternatives.

FEAR: Lifting weights will jeopardize my pregnancy.

FEARLESS FACT: Light weightlifting is actually great for a pregnancy.

An old wives' tale was that lifting your arms over your head would cause something undesirable to happen to the umbilical cord. Luckily, we aren't that gullible; otherwise, we might not blow-dry our hair, right? But the notion still persists that lifting weighty objects (and this includes dumbbells) is a pregnancy felony. It's not even a misdemeanor.

In fact, weightlifting is great for you because it'll maintain your muscle tone and it isn't jarring. Don't lift to the point at which you're out of breath or otherwise overexerting yourself (you should probably keep your weights at under twenty-five pounds), but that said, lift away.

Exercise Scale-down

Even if you're in top condition, you'll likely need to scale down your exercise program during pregnancy. In the first trimester, for example, you may be dealing with nausea and extreme fatigue, both of which could limit your workout ability. Later in your pregnancy, your center of gravity will change, which affects your balance.

That said, if you're an avid exerciser, keep it up. The only thing you have to remember is to stay away from extreme sports or from activities where there's a good chance you'll fall or get hit in the stomach. Otherwise, stick with what you've been doing and make small adjustments along the way as your pregnancy progresses. The chart on the following pages shows examples of sensible ways to alter three different exercise programs so that you can work out healthfully and safely through the whole pregnancy.

Exercise Scale-down

WHAT HAPPENS	HOW TO ADJUST
First Trimester Nausea, fatigue, and dizziness may present problems.	***Kick Boxing*** FIRST TRIMESTER: • Alter to low-impact (reduced bouncing/jumping). • Stop if you become nauseated, dizzy, or overheated. • Temporarily scale back frequency if you're battling fatigue.
Second Trimester Balance could be compromised because of the changing center of gravity that accompanies a growing midsection.	SECOND TRIMESTER: (All of the above, plus...) • Widen stance for better balance. • Switch from floor-based ab exercises to standing leg lifts or ab exercises on a 45-degree-angle step. • Limit aerobic workout to 30 minutes.
Third Trimester The amount of blood circulated by the heart will be about 30 to 50 percent above normal. This means you'll use more oxygen for the same exercise intensity.	THIRD TRIMESTER: (All of the above, plus...) • Keep kicks low to floor and reduce snap of punches (reduces heart rate). • Eliminate floor exercises on your back (do wall squats, standing leg lifts, or cat stretches on all fours).

HOW TO ADJUST	HOW TO ADJUST
Yoga	***Treadmill Running***
FIRST TRIMESTER: • Use a wall to reduce dizziness/instability in inversions, tree pose, etc. • Take gentle yoga classes if battling fatigue.	FIRST TRIMESTER: • Consider interspersing walking if battling nausea. • Stop if you become queasy, dizzy, or overheated. • Temporarily scale back frequency if you're battling fatigue.
SECOND TRIMESTER: (All of the above, plus...) • Consider switching to prenatal classes. • Widen stance to hip-width for poses such as mountain pose. • Switch from backbends to bridges. • Switch from upward dogs/cobras to cat stretches. • Reverse all twists (twist away from baby).	SECOND TRIMESTER: (All of the above, plus...) • Slow your running to reduce impact, or walk. • Limit aerobic workout to 30 minutes.
THIRD TRIMESTER: (All of the above, plus...) • Switch to prenatal or gentle yoga classes.	THIRD TRIMESTER: (All of the above, plus...) • Switch to recumbent bike for better stability.

~ *Fast and Fearless*

Here's all you need to know about diet, weight gain, and exercise:

- Unless you starve yourself (a very serious no-no) or binge, the amount you gain is pretty much genetically predetermined. Don't compare yourself with others or with what's "officially" recommended; your doctor or midwife will tell you if you're gaining too much or too little.
- Eat frequently (six small meals a day, ideally), but also realize you need an average of only 300 calories more per day during pregnancy.
- Don't deny your cravings; indulge but try not to go wild.
- If you currently exercise, try to keep it up (although you might need to scale back a tad as you grow). Your gym friends will be in awe of you, and it'll be a big—and sometimes much needed—ego boost.
- Keep your heart rate moderate, drink plenty of water, and avoid insanely risky sports (you don't want to fall or get kicked in the stomach).
- Abdominal exercises are fine, but there will be a point at which you won't want to do them anymore.
- If you don't currently exercise, there's no harm in starting to walk regularly, taking a pregnancy yoga class, or trying some other enjoyable program. It will make you feel better; we promise.

5

Fearless Maternity Fashion

"When I first got pregnant I dreaded the day I'd have to put on maternity pants. But once I hit the stores and found out what maternity clothes look like these days I was pleasantly surprised. You can be pregnant, still look pretty hip and not spend a fortune!"

— Jen, mother of 9-month-old Sarah.

FEAR: I won't be able to wear any of my normal clothes.

FEARLESS FACT: You'll be able to wear some, but not most.

Some women still think that once they become pregnant, they'll be forced into 100 percent maternity wear. That's not true at all. My friend Kathryn didn't have to buy one maternity item throughout either of her pregnancies. Of course, that's because she's really into those flowing, loose-fitting dresses, and she looks good in them. Not everyone can or wants to wear those. But most women will be surprised to find that there are some items in their closets that work well.

What works for you will depend on what you're comfortable wearing and what size you wear (before pregnancy and during). Here are some ideas of where to look. Any pants with drawstrings and wide, loose elastic bands often work until the bitter end for many women (the current yoga- and workout-inspired fashions are perfect). And this may sound crazy, but I've even known women who've worn nonmaternity pajama bottoms as maternity pants. True, these were more the loungewear type in sedate colors such as black or navy, but they worked.

Overalls and babydoll-style tops and dresses also do it for some women. Don't just think big, though. Stretchy jersey skirts (sometimes worn below the belly) look great on many pregnant bodies. I got lots of mileage out of a pair of form-fitting black, boot-cut workout pants during my pregnancy. I also wore nonmaternity, stretchy, form-fitting tee-shirts, cotton/spandex tanks with built-in shelf bras, and nylon tops. I'm not sure what an environmentalist would say about it, but I feel spandex (and other stretchy, man-made fibers) has, in general, been a blessing to the entire human race—and particularly to pregnant women.

Say Goodbye, but Not for Long

Sometime around the beginning of your second trimester (or before), you must raid your closet and do some rearranging. The objective is to ferret out what could possibly be wearable and to bury what definitely won't. This is a good idea because then you can clearly see what you'll have to wear before you hit a crisis point, and you won't have to torture yourself by looking at all your cute, nonpregnant clothes.

I put all jeans, pants, and skirts with defined waists immediately to the back of my closet. I also said goodbye to fitted jackets and shirts. Don't worry, they'll come back one day not so far away. If you own a lot of extremely trendy clothes, however, you may want to consider offering to loan them to friends. If your wardrobe is still stylish enough to be wearable when you're able to fit into it again, your friends can give everything back. This may sound a little depressing, but it's practical. At least somebody will get some use out of your trendy things while they're still current. Besides, with so many nice and affordable maternity clothes available now, you'll have plenty of fun stuff to wear. Maybe you won't even miss your old duds.

FEAR: I'll go broke on maternity clothes.

FEARLESS FACT: No you won't, thanks to major chains getting into the action.

It used to be that maternity clothes were costly and ugly. Now, thankfully, neither is true, as long as you choose wisely. Check out Target as well as Old Navy and Gap. Motherhood Maternity is also extremely reasonable. You'll obviously get the most mileage for your money if you buy basics such as a pair of black pants, a pair of jeans, and a couple of simple tees. I bought three pregnancy tanks with built-in shelf bras (black, white, and blue), a pair of black maternity pants, and a beige zip-up sweater jacket. These, along with the wearable nonpregnant items I already owned (skirts and drawstring pants), were my staples and got me through most of the pregnancy.

Sharewear

Maternity clothing is not really worth saving in case you have another baby. Usually, by the time that happens, the clothing will be outdated. Also, the chances are that your babies will be born in different seasons, so the sweaters and turtlenecks you wore for your first January baby won't work for your second July one.

Instead of allowing maternity clothes to take up your undoubtedly valuable closet space, be a pal and pass them along to another pregnant sister. If someone has allowed you to borrow her pregnancy clothing, return it clean and folded as soon as possible so she can pass it along to someone else.

Yes, eBay!

My niece Jen was brilliant when she figured out this one. She wanted a certain style of maternity jeans but didn't want to pay full price. Instead, she logged on to eBay, did a search, and presto! She was able to buy the very jeans she wanted for half price. The seller even threw in a shirt. Of course, the clothing was used, but it was in great shape, and it arrived at her door in days. Here are Jen's tips for maternity shopping on eBay:

- Visit your favorite maternity store and try on clothes to figure out what you like. Jen discovered, for example, that boot-cut jeans looked best on her.
- Do an eBay search based on what you learned in the store. You can search by brand or type of clothing (such as Gap maternity jeans, boot-cut jeans, Pea in the Pod maternity wear, etc.).
- Buy from nonsmoking households. The clothes just smell better.
- Read the details. If there's a stain or hole, it should be disclosed. If the condition of the garment isn't mentioned, email the seller and ask.

Don't Try to Outsmart the Blue Jean Goddess
(or the Black or Tan Jean Goddess, for that matter)

I thought I was being very thrifty and smart by buying some of those old-lady (sorry Mom), elastic waistband jeans at Target for $10 and wearing them during my pregnancy. I bought them a size bigger than normal, and they did look surprisingly good for the most part. However, around the eighth month, they were no longer comfortable, and I broke down and bought some real maternity jeans.

Other women I've known have tried to avoid maternity jeans by using a rubber band to secure the button on their normal jeans or by wearing their partner's pants. All of these strategies end in the same miserable way: they stop working, and you break down and buy maternity jeans.

The truth is, maternity jeans should not be feared. They are surprisingly stylish and reasonable, and best of all, they fit big, pregnant bellies! So if you normally like jeans, do yourself a favor and buy these early. You'll get plenty of wear and tear out of them, and you won't have to subject yourself to the aforementioned humiliation and misery.

Cheap Can Be Chic Too

If you have money to burn on maternity wear, you will find plenty of boutiques and online stores. But for pregnancy, most of us can get by with cheaper clothing that's still fun. Target, K-Mart, Wal-Mart, Old Navy, and the Gap are excellent sources for drawstring pants that will work through your entire pregnancy and for the months afterward when you're trying to shed the weight. You can also find inexpensive maternity clothes at these stores.

One warning, though: some women have complained that the cheaper stuff tends to shrink. So either wash it carefully or buy it a little bigger. For stretchy tops, hit the sales racks at inexpensive teeny-bopper stores. Sometimes you can find funky and fashionable nylon tops that will stretch over pregnant bellies and look great for as little as $5. None of this bargain shopping is as fun as buying designer stuff, but you could do something phenomenal with your savings—like starting a college fund for your kid or saving for a "babymoon" (a family bonding vacation sometime after the baby is born).

The Baby Shower Outfit

Yes, you're going to need a flattering outfit for your baby shower. By the time the shower rolls around, you're going to be pretty big. So plan ahead. If there's a casual wedding, a party, or another special event coming up, you may want to buy a maternity outfit you love and wear it to these events and also to your shower. Don't, as many of us have done, panic a few days before the shower, buy a new outfit, and then get limited mileage out of it.

FEAR: I'm going to have to wear a tent.

FEARLESS FACT: It's fashionable to be pregnant and show it.

Things have really changed in the last few years regarding covering up versus showing the pregnant belly. I think we can trace this back, at least partially, to Demi Moore's pregnant *Vanity Fair* cover. Once she showed off that belly, pregnant women everywhere said what the heck. Now it is not uncommon to see pregnant women completely exposing their bellies, whether it's at the gym or in a restaurant. Of course, this is a highly personal choice. Many women would never do this (or they feel they can't because their bellies look mottled or have stretch marks). But if you have the moxie to do it, I say go for it.

A modified version of this idea is to wear a sheer nylon top with a tank or bra underneath so that your belly is visible but not entirely exposed. You could also wear shirts that show a peek of the skin but not everything. Sometimes a stretchy, nonmaternity tee will give you this look. You can even layer a cardigan or jacket over a top for more discretion. Do whatever comes naturally, but don't think you have to hide anything.

Baring It All

Nude or partially nude pregnancy photographs are gaining in popularity. Again, this trend must have been spurred by Demi Moore and other pregnant celebrities who have posed for magazines.

If you're going to have these photos taken, it's best to do it around your seventh month. You'll be big, but not too big. Of course, you may look phenomenal throughout your entire pregnancy. But for most women the chance that they'll have swollen ankles, trouble sleeping, and other obstacles that may lead to less-than-perfect photos increases during the last few months.

What About Under Your Clothes?

Bikini-style underwear works best in pregnancy because it's already designed to be worn low, below the belly. Many women buy cotton bikinis one size larger than normal, and this works throughout the entire pregnancy. If you don't like wearing bikinis, you should probably invest in maternity underwear. That way, they'll fit in the front and the back. One of my friends broke down and bought maternity underwear her last six weeks or so of pregnancy, and she said she wished she had bought it from the start because it was so comfortable. Of course, the briefs may look like "granny panties," but sometimes your happiness, not how you look, must take precedence.

Bras are a trickier matter. Most women's breasts get bigger, but for some women it's not a drastic change. They're able to continue wearing their normal bras or a stretchy tank with a built-in bra that they wear underneath their shirts. For others, it's an unbelievable change. Their breasts become huge. If you're in the latter category, it's a good idea to visit a maternity or breast-feeding store. Someone will measure you and advise you on the best size to purchase. Armed with this information, you can also buy bras online for less, and they'll arrive in days.

Generally, you'll wind up buying a nursing bra. It's not a waste, though, because you can also wear this postpartum at least for a while (even if you don't nurse). Most breast-feeding pros, however, don't recommend underwires because they seem to promote clogged milk ducts. These bras are best avoided, even if you feel you need the extra support. If you're bigger breasted, you'll also likely need to wear a stretchy sports bra or a sleep-bra at night (available at maternity shops or online). Again, you'll also want to keep these to wear postpartum.

Swimwear

The jury is out on whether it's a good idea to buy a maternity swimsuit. If it's summertime, if you'll be in the pool often, and if you like to be discreet, go ahead. On the other hand, I wore my normal tankini, and as I grew, I just progressively showed more stomach.

FEAR: I'm going to look like a fashion "don't."

FEARLESS FACT: Top designers are now churning out chic pregnancy wear.

You don't have to be a fashionista to realize that there's extremely cool maternity wear out there. Whatever your style, you can find it. The only thing you have to understand is the same thing you have to keep in mind when you're shopping for nonpregnant clothes. Those are models you see in the advertisements and magazines. They may be pregnant, but they are still models. Most pregnant models would look good in a burlap sack, but they look phenomenal with the help of expert photographers, stylists, makeup artists, and hair people, not to mention those computer photo retouching pros. So, repeat after me: Pregnant models do not look like real pregnant people no matter how fashionable the clothing.

Skip the Makeovers

Image pros advise clients not to cut their hair off or make drastic changes during times of stress and upheaval. This is good advice for pregnancy too. Being pregnant is enough of a change. So when (or if) you're considering your pregnancy "look," it's best to stick to something similar to how you normally look. If you typically wear tailored skirts and jackets, for example, it would be bizarre to suddenly start wearing flowing hippie dresses. Your friends will think the pregnancy hormones have really done a number on you, and you probably won't feel like yourself. The point is to try to feel as comfortable and normal as possible. The clothes you wear can go a long way toward this, or they can have the opposite effect.

Footnote

I love the maternity clothing ads that show models in high-heels looking as cute as can be. You may be able to wear heels and boots at the beginning of your pregnancy, but midway through you will probably be reduced to flats. By the end, you may even be dining further down the footwear food chain: flip flops and stretched-out tennis shoes!

I'm just warning you in case you wake up one morning, put on a nice outfit, and then discover your feet are a tad swollen and none of your decent shoes fit. If you show up at work or a party with old, stretched-out Birkenstocks, just issue a disclaimer upon entering. Nobody holds fashion atrocities against pregnant women.

Buy Your Style Online

Many of the brands you like in nonpregnant life may have maternity versions, but those probably aren't sold at the retail outlet. You may have to purchase them online. However, they should be close to the price you normally pay and close to the style of clothes you generally wear.

~ *Fast and Fearless*

Here's all you need to know about maternity fashion:

- Nonmaternity yoga- and exercise-inspired workout pants perform really well for many women. Nylon tops and stretchy tees and skirts are also good bets.
- For maximum mileage on maternity wear, think basics first: black pants, tees, tanks, and a sweater jacket. Consider buying a special event outfit too, especially if you're having a shower.
- And, yes, jeans! Don't mess around; just buy yourself a pair of maternity jeans early on and gets lots of wear out of them.
- Of course, if friends offer to lend you their maternity clothes, take them. Pass along your own stash as soon as possible.

- Major chains such as Target, Old Navy (oldnavy.com), and Gap (gap.com) now have fashionable maternity wear at unbeatable prices (but be prepared for shrinkage on some items).
- Shop online and even eBay. Sometimes you'll get great loot at half off.
- Regarding footwear, don't be surprised if you can only wear flip-flops and stretched-out sandals or tennis shoes by the end (sorry, but that's the truth).
- If money isn't an issue, go wild; there are some incredibly cute maternity clothes nowadays.

6

Fearless (Pregnant) Living

"When I found out I was pregnant, suddenly everything seemed dangerous. I started raiding the closet and looking at my skin care products, worrying about what I'd drunk or eaten before I knew, and freaking out about the fact that I'd even been around smoke."

– Karen, sixteen weeks pregnant

FEAR: What might happen because of what I did in my life before I knew I was pregnant?

FEARLESS FACT: In the first weeks of conception, very little can harm a viable pregnancy.

Just before I found out I was pregnant, we celebrated my husband's birthday and our wedding anniversary with a trip out of town. What did we do? Martinis, sushi, a few trips into smoke-filled bars, a trip on a plane full of germs! Of course, when I found out I was pregnant, I started scanning my brain for any and all so-called transgressions.

This is pretty common. When my friend Karen discovered she was pregnant, she phoned her doctor several times asking, What if I went to a concert? What if I was exposed to smoke? She even paged him when she found out that the rash one of her clients had (she's a licensed massage therapist) was scabies. She was panicked.

Obstetricians must be blessed with an extremely large dose of patience, because just think how hellish their lives must be having to call each one of us back about these issues. I've been told, too, that these types of calls are pretty much constant throughout the day for doctors and midwives. I will save you the phone call (and save your doctor or midwife a little time perhaps): Mother Nature has ensured that during the first weeks of the pregnancy the fetus is ultraprotected because cells are merely dividing, not forming organs.

Don't worry about smoking, drinking, or almost anything you did beforehand, but be honest with your practitioner. If you did hard drugs or have other concerns, let him or her know. You likely have nothing to worry about.

Of course, now that you know you're pregnant, you're not going to booze it up, smoke, stay up all night, or go all day without eating! That's not being fearless; that's being negligent.

Risks and Living

FEARLESS DOC

Our choices of what we do in life, whether pregnant or not, always come down to risk versus benefit. For instance, the risk of getting out of bed each morning is that you might slip and fall, have a car accident, or argue with a co-worker. These are what we call *theoretical* risks. In theory, yes, these acts pose a risk, but nobody has quantified how much of a risk. Most of us believe either it's a long-shot risk or, if something does happen, that life will still go on. Besides, we want the benefits: being able to go to the bathroom, drive a car, earn a paycheck, and so on. We take risks every day, and that will continue while you're pregnant.

The funny thing is, I have pregnant women constantly ask me about things in life that pose very minor theoretical risks (hair color or certain foods, for example), but I've never had a pregnant woman ask me if she should stop driving. For most of us, driving is our most dangerous daily activity. And yet, we need to go places, so we continue—as we should.

The bottom line is that pregnant women are bombarded with precautions and warnings about the dangers of living in our world, and for the most part the precautions and warnings are absolutely overblown and unnecessary. We're just not so fragile a species, you and I, that the so-called perils of everyday life should be a worry.

Smoking

FEARLESS DOC

If you smoke, you should try your best to quit while you're pregnant. The reality is, however, that an occasional cigarette (say one cigarette a week) probably won't have any impact on your pregnancy. But regular smoking, of course, has been linked to premature and low-birth-weight babies. It's also not advisable to breathe a lot of second-hand smoke on a consistent basis, either. But, again, an occasional whiff is not going to do in you or your child.

Sex and Pregnancy

FEAR: Having sex will disturb my baby.

FEARLESS FACT: If you enjoy it, so will your baby.

Sex during pregnancy is perfectly fine as long as your doctor or midwife hasn't told you specifically to abstain. Yet I think it would be overly optimistic to suggest that most pregnant women will have raging sex lives. It's possible, not probable.

Many women report that their sex drives shrink as they grow. And many male partners also lose their zest for sex as the delivery date nears. Why? Sometimes it's a logistical matter. It's really hard to maneuver as you get bigger. But more often, there's a psychological component to it. Sometimes there's a feeling that the baby is getting jostled or disturbed. Rest assured, this isn't happening. If you're having sex, your baby is happy about it. That's how he got where he is!

When Sex Is a Pain

FEARLESS Midwife

Occasionally women have more desire for sex during pregnancy. But more commonly, they find that intercourse isn't always as comfortable as it was before. Sometimes a woman's cervix or vagina is more sensitive, and any pressure is perceived as pain. If this is the case, this may be the time in your relationship to find other ways to achieve sexual satisfaction for both of you.

WHEN *NOT* TO HAVE SEX

Barring any complications of pregnancy or possible transmission of STDs, sex is usually safe throughout the entire pregnancy. But there are also certain times during your pregnancy that you should not engage in sexual activity without getting clearance from your health care provider. Ask specific questions about what activity is allowed. For a woman, nipple stimulation, orgasm, and intercourse can all trigger contractions of the uterus. So if your health care provider says "no sex," he or she may mean more than just intercourse.

The following situations (as well as those mentioned previously) are times when you should **not** engage in any sexual activity, unless you have approval:

- Pre-term labor or contractions
- Rupture of membranes (mother's water has broken)
- Vaginal bleeding
- Risk of sexually transmitted disease or vaginal infection (unless treatment has been completed by both partners when indicated and/or condoms are used)
- After amniocentesis (abstain for 72 hours)
- After CVS (abstain for two weeks)

FEAR: I'll never want sex again after the baby.

FEARLESS FACT: It'll take time, but eventually you'll get your sizzle back.

You'll get the green light for sex six weeks postpartum, but after everything your body and mind will go through during pregnancy and delivery, it's reasonable to fear you might not want to have sex for a lot longer than that. And the first, third, or fourth time you have sex after the baby comes, you may also question whether you really want to ever have it again. But don't worry, because, yes, you will eventually dust off your sex life. Don't we all know women who have back-to-back babies?

If you want to plan ahead, buy some K-Y Jelly (think of this as your new, postpartum, sexy lingerie). Lubrication will be essential because you are likely to be a bit sore the first few times, and if you're breast-feeding, the decreased estrogen will cause vaginal dryness. Also, as you might imagine, it's difficult to feel sexy when you're covered with spit-up, you're up at all hours, and your breasts are leaking.

An even bigger obstacle, however, may be the little thing sleeping in the bassinet next to your bed. As if having an extra person in the bedroom isn't enough of a romantic hindrance, when family and friends offer to watch newborns, they tend to want to do it at your home where all supplies are easily accessible. All this makes a sex life more tricky, but not impossible. One of my friends and her husband actually borrowed her sister's apartment for some mommy and daddy alone time. You'll have to hang in there and get creative if you need to, but eventually your sex life should get back on track.

Libido Worries?

FEARLESS DOC

Many women find that for some time after they have a baby, they have no libido. This is absolutely normal and has everything to do with evolution and little to do with you. A decreased postpartum sex drive is due to decreased ovarian hormone production—mainly androgens (the key hormones that make you interested in sex). The female body is designed like this to guarantee the survival of the species. It wouldn't serve the human species well for a woman to give birth and then get pregnant again immediately. There's a concerted need to nurture and protect a helpless baby for a year or two before Mother Nature wants you to divide your resources by having another one.

That said, all women are different; some will have their libidos return more quickly than others. If you ever have questions about your sex drive at any point, bring them up with your doctor or midwife and get answers. This is far better than allowing the issue to have a negative impact on your relationship.

Postpartum Sex and Your Guy

Many guys say their friends tell them that once they have a baby, their wives don't want sex anymore. Those friends, though, don't seem to tell them why—that is, the physical reasons why women aren't gung-ho about sex for some time afterward. Maybe they don't know, but you do, and you should clue your partner in. He'll likely have more understanding and suffer fewer blows to his ego.

On the other hand, don't be surprised if he isn't as interested in sex as usual. Men can also suffer from newborn exhaustion and the psychological weight of being a new dad.

If You Have Sex Soon Afterward...

FEARLESS Midwife

Occasionally, I'll have a patient who comes in for her six-week postpartum visit and has already resumed sex. If your bleeding has stopped (usually this takes two to six weeks) and you really want to have sex, that's fine. But I highly recommend using a condom. Why?

Six-weeks postpartum is usually when the issue of birth control is addressed. Even if you are not having your period yet, do not assume you can't get pregnant. You can! If you have unprotected sex, we can't put you on birth control or insert an IUD until we're sure you're not pregnant. It just makes it all much more complicated. So wait, or at the very least use a condom.

Is Breast-feeding Safe When You're Pregnant?

Okay, let's say you did have unprotected sex fairly quickly after giving birth, and here you are pregnant while you're still breast-feeding the first one. Unless you're having problems with pre-term labor, it's perfectly safe to breast-feed another baby or toddler while pregnant. Some women, though, find that their nipples are too tender, and they decide to wean. Other times, your child will naturally wean because the taste of breast milk changes during pregnancy.

~ *Fast and Fearless*

Here's everything you need to know about sex and pregnancy:

- Your baby doesn't mind if you have sex.
- You can have sex throughout your pregnancy, unless your doctor has told you to abstain. If you're told to abstain, also avoid nipple stimulation.
- Don't be surprised if sex becomes uncomfortable for your partner or you. Pregnancy can be physically and psychologically challenging, which sometimes negatively affects your sex life.
- You *will* have a sex life again, although it may take longer than you think to get it back (count on at least a few months postpartum, and buy some K-Y Jelly).

FEAR: I'll have to let my hair go natural.

FEARLESS FACT: There's plenty you can do with hair products to damage your hair, but not much you can do to damage the baby.

Yes, this is enough to scare many women out of their wits. We all remember Madonna when she was pregnant—the black-root look. And many of us probably assumed she couldn't color her hair, because that's what we're often told. But Madonna must've wanted her hair that way. Because the truth is, there isn't any proven risk to coloring your hair while you're pregnant. In fact, there isn't any proven risk to getting a permanent or other hair treatments, either.

But there is a theoretical risk. When chemicals are put on the scalp, a small amount is absorbed through the skin. As I said, there isn't any proven risk, but some women (maybe Madonna) decide *au naturel* is fine, particularly in the first trimester when the organs are forming. If you're paranoid, but need to do something for your hair, highlight. That doesn't even touch your scalp.

On Hair Color

FEARLESS DOC Coloring your hair poses a theoretical risk that has never been quantified. My belief is that it's probably safe, but I recommend to my patients that, if possible, they avoid it for at least the first trimester when the baby's organs are forming.

Many people think coloring your hair is all about vanity, but often that's not the whole story. There are women whose income or activities depend on their appearance, such as media personalities or actresses. They have to weigh the minuscule, unknown risk versus the benefit to their careers and future, which will be important for the support of their child.

Don't Skip Your Teeth

Some women assume they shouldn't have any dental care during their pregnancy, but this is absolutely wrong. It's extremely important to maintain your regular checkups and cleanings, at the least. Pregnancy hormones put you more at risk for gingivitis. That's why cleaning is important, and it's also why you may notice puffy gums or bleeding. Don't worry, though, because this goes away soon after delivery. Most major dental work will be put off until after you deliver, if it can. If it can't be put off, it's still true that dental work is generally safe, although it may not be the most comfortable thing to sit through when you're eight months pregnant.

On Sun Worshipping

Dermatologists will tell you that for your skin's health and your own long-term well-being, you shouldn't use a tanning booth or lie in the sun. But for your baby's health, there's no reason you can't. Common sense says use moderation. Being sunburned and pregnant will not be comfortable. Also, if you're out in the sun, drink plenty of water to avoid dehydration. It's also fine—advisable, in fact—to use sunscreen products.

Hold the High-Tech Beauty

FEARLESS Midwife

Many women use beauty products such as Retin-A, get laser treatments and have wrinkle-fighting procedures such as Botox and Restylane injections. If you've done any of this before realizing you're pregnant, don't worry. Your baby will be fine. None of these are known to be harmful. Still, I do recommend against continuing to use them while you're pregnant. Remember, you only have about 40 weeks to be pregnant; you can spend the rest of your life worrying about laugh lines.

> It's certain that use of Accutane (an acne-fighting drug) is contraindicated while pregnant. Talk to your practitioner right away if you're on this drug and you become pregnant.

FEAR: A pedicure may cause contractions.

FEARLESS FACT: The average pedicure is harmless.

When you're really pregnant and probably can't even see your toes, you'll be struck with the desire to have a pedicure. At least I was (as were many other pregnant women I know). I think it's reasonable to want your toes to look spiffy, even though you may feel less than spiffy yourself, but this becomes essential the week or so before delivery. We all want our toes delivery room ready, right?

When I went to get the pedicure, I announced to the nail technician, "I'm pregnant!" (as if she couldn't tell). She stared at me with a very blank expression and said, "Uh, yeah." I explained that I thought I should let her know because I vaguely remembered reading somewhere that pedicures might be inadvisable. She nearly fell off her stool laughing before she pointed out that she had three children—and that all of her clients probably had at least one.

In fact, you may notice that nail shops are a haven for pregnant women. It's something you can do to feel and look better instantly. Also, all the workers like to guess whether you're going to have a boy or girl, how big the baby will be, etc. There's absolutely nothing wrong with the normal pedicure—or manicure, for that matter. It'll amount to getting your hands or feet scrubbed and massaged and having your nails groomed and painted. This will make you feel good, but not good enough to send you into labor.

Foot Reflexology

A foot reflexology session is different from a pedicure. Foot reflexology is an ancient holistic practice based on the belief that the sole contains reflex points that link to all areas of the body. It's sort of like acupressure for the foot. Although there isn't much research on foot reflexology's benefits or risks, most practitioners avoid working on pregnant women.

A Day at the Spa

Many spas advertise maternal bliss treatments and other services for pregnant women. Are they safe? For the most part, yes. You can have all the manicures, pedicures, and facials you want (or, rather, can afford). Massages, water therapy, or other body treatments are also quite safe, but here are a few guidelines to consider:

~ **Ask about training.** Make sure your masseuse or therapist has been trained in pregnancy massage. There are no state or federally mandated requirements, but just the knowledge that they have specific training will help ensure that they're sensitive to expectant moms and will be more likely to have your comfort in mind.

~ **Avoid too much heat.** Most doctors recommend against raising your body temperature excessively during pregnancy. So skip the pre- and post-treatment steam room and sauna. Body wraps are also off limits. You can dangle your feet in the Jacuzzi, though, and individual hydrotherapy treatments are fine if the water temperature isn't too hot (close to body temperature is ideal).

~ **Be scent cautious.** Common fragrances such as lavender, grapefruit, or eucalyptus aren't harmful but could make you queasy. If you've been sensitive to smells in general, ask for scent-free products.

~ **Listen to your body.** Let your therapist know if you're uncomfortable. Positioning isn't usually an issue during the first trimester, but as the pregnancy progresses, it's much more important. Some spas use tables with cutouts to accommodate a pregnant belly, but the trend is toward prenatal support pillows because they are more adjustable and generally more comfortable. Since every woman and each stage of pregnancy is different, however, even with the pillows you may not be comfortable, particularly on your belly or your back. If not, ask to switch positions or otherwise alter the treatment. Also, speak up if you have to use the bathroom—even if it's in the middle of a service.

- **Eat and drink.** You're supposed to relax, but don't get so relaxed that you forget to drink plenty of water and have a snack.

ROYAL TREATMENT AT PEASANT PRICES

Spa treatments are great, but it's the very ambiance of these places that's "therapeutic." Think candles, warm robes, soothing music. If you'd like to soak it up but can't shell out $75 or more for many of the treatments, look for a local day spa (or a nice hotel with a spa) and book something inexpensive, such as a pedicure or manicure. Even with a $25 service, you'll still get to use the amenities for a few hours. Just sitting by the pool or in the waiting room (sometimes called the "meditation room") in your nice comfy robe and spa slippers can be fun and relaxing.

The Beauty Myth

Forget the glow of pregnancy. The truth is, pregnant women suffer unpredictable changes in their appearances. Skin, for example, may become flawless, but it's also just as likely to break out, become unbearably dry and itchy, or get splotchy or otherwise discolored. Your hair and nails may get long and strong—or they may not. Each woman is different, and the impact the pregnancy hormones have on your appearance is completely unpredictable.

If you have a skin problem, don't be afraid to visit your dermatologist. There are often perfectly safe services or medications that will help ease your situation. And the very best beauty advice is something you'll hear often in pregnancy: Know that you won't be pregnant forever.

Nail Fumes?

FEARLESS DOC

Going into a nail shop to have your nails done while you're pregnant won't cause you or your baby harm, even if the shop stinks inside because of the products used there. You'd need massive and long-term exposure to the products before you'd have any chance of a problem (even then it's questionable). That's why you see pregnant nail technicians still on the job.

There is one problem you could encounter, though. The fumes might make you queasy. Pregnant women are more sensitive to scents. If this is a problem, frequent a shop that has good ventilation, or at least get your nails done first thing in the morning before the place gets buzzing.

Sickness and Health in Pregnancy

FEAR: The cold medicine I took may cause birth defects.

FEARLESS FACT: Almost all over-the-counter medications (ditto for many prescription meds) will not harm your developing baby.

Even though it's standard to see the words "pregnant and lactating women should consult their physician before taking this" on over-the-counter remedies from antacids to flu medicine, the truth is that once you consult your doctor, you'll be told it's safe to take them. In fact, it's usually better to treat problems rather than suffer. Anything that makes you healthier and happier is generally good for your baby.

When I was pregnant, I had an extremely bad cold and cough. I managed to lose my voice and spend about five days in bed before I finally called my doctor. Why? I firmly believed, as most pregnant women do, that I couldn't and shouldn't take a thing! I was promptly informed that I should get to the drugstore for Robitussin and Sudafed.

It was nice that I was trying to be a trooper, but a severe cough could conceivably put unnecessary pressure on the cervix. Even with this unnecessary pressure, the odds that anything bad would've happened are small, but it just illustrates the point that you're *not* being a better expectant mom by suffering through a cold, cough, or flu without medicine. There are no benefits, and there may be some drawbacks.

Treating Illnesses During Pregnancy

Although you may think it's best not to take any sort of medication during pregnancy, that's not really accurate. The medication may actually allow your pregnancy to progress better. Here's an example: A study in the journal

Obstetrics and Gynecology found that untreated or under-treated asthma was a greater risk to the fetus and newborn than were the medications used to manage the problem. So breathe easy if your doctor prescribes medication.

From the Fearless Doc:

What to Take for Common Illnesses While Pregnant

At some point during your pregnancy, you're likely to catch a cold, have diarrhea or vomiting, get a headache, or develop a rash. Count on this, because ailments that are common to all of us can be expected to afflict us in pregnancy as well.

Many women believe they can't take anything because they're pregnant. Nothing could be further from the truth! *As a general rule, it's safe for pregnant women to take almost all over-the-counter remedies.* You will not harm your baby by taking medicines that give you relief. I routinely recommend these over-the-counter medicines, which are quite safe during pregnancy:

- Tylenol for headaches, fever, and body aches
- Imodium for diarrhea
- Milk of Magnesia or Metamucil for constipation
- Robitussin for coughs
- TheraFlu or Nyquil for colds
- Sudafed or Benadryl for congestion or allergies
- Medicated lozenges for sore throats
- Mylanta or Tums for heartburn (also known as reflux)
- Anusol or Tucks for hemorrhoids (which are especially common in the later weeks of pregnancy)

Some problems may not resolve with over-the-counter treatments, and your practitioner may want you to take a prescription medication.

Rest assured that there are many prescriptions that are known to be safe for pregnant women, and your doctor will know which ones they are. Many have been screened intensely by the Food and Drug Administration for use during pregnancy.

For personal reasons, you may not want to take anything while you're pregnant. This is a noble goal, but just know that most medicines, when needed, will help you get better faster, and that's good for both you and your baby.

PRESCRIPTION MEDICATIONS

In my practice, there are some prescription medications that I have commonly used for many years, and I feel confident endorsing their safety. These include:

- Ampicillin, Penicillin, Zithromax, Keflex, and Macrobid for infections
- Zofran, Compazine, Reglan, or Phenergan for severe morning sickness
- Valtrex, Zovirax, and Famvir for herpes prophylaxis and treatment
- Protonix, Prevacid, and Nexium for GERD (gastroesophageal reflux disease)
- Ativan, Halcion, Ambien, and Sonata for sleep
- Aldomet, Catapres, Hydralazine, and Labetalol for high blood pressure
- Zyrtec for allergies

MEDICATIONS FOR ONGOING DISORDERS

Some women are on long-term medication for disorders such as hypothyroidism, diabetes, or asthma. There is no need to fear, although some adjustment in your dosage may be necessary as your body changes over the nine months. If you have a rather rare medical condition requiring other types of medications and therapies not mentioned here, rest assured that almost all of these remedies will be safe to continue in pregnancy. Of course, you should consult your physician to make sure no changes need to occur.

There are some medications, however, that are absolutely contraindicated, although they are the exception. Ideally, a discussion with your doctor should take place before you become pregnant. If, however, you happen to be on a medication for a few weeks before you realize you're pregnant, it's important to remember the following general rule: The first few weeks after conception are a rather protected time for the developing embryo. It's extremely unlikely that anything you take during this time can affect the development or outcome of your pregnancy. Nature was very smart in protecting babies this way.

TREATING DEPRESSION SAFELY

If you were diagnosed with depression and prescribed an antidepressant before you became pregnant, you will most likely need to continue treatment. This is the best advice for you and your baby's health. In my practice, I feel comfortable with patients on Prozac, Celexa, Paxil, Wellbutrin, Effexor, and LexiPro. I don't recommend herbal treatments such as St. John's wort or SAM-E because there hasn't been a lot of research on their safety and/or efficacy in pregnancy. Follow the advice of your practitioner.

Herbs and Pregnancy

Herbal remedies are becoming so prevalent that some doctors' and hospitals' admitting questionnaires have been changed to explicitly ask women to list any herb and complementary or alternative remedy they may have taken. But you shouldn't wait to be asked. Your doctor or midwife needs to know if you're taking any herb or supplement. Common herbs such as St. John's wort, echinacea, and gingko, for example, all have the potential to interfere with medications used during or after delivery.

Environmental Hazards during Pregnancy

FEAR: Toxins leached by plastic containers will cause deformities.

FEARLESS FACT: Most plastics are fine.

When I was pregnant, a study published in the journal *Current Biology* found that mice exposed to a chemical present in certain plastics used to make some water jugs, plastic kitchenware, and even baby bottles and children's sippy cups had "highly significant" increases in abnormalities in their developing eggs. In humans, the researchers said, these kinds of chromosomal abnormalities were a leading cause of miscarriage, congenital defects, and mental retardation.

Overall, it's terrific that researchers are doing these studies, because they may learn that it's better for the entire human species and our environment to use some materials and not use others. And in the best case, their studies will put pressure on manufacturers to use the safest possible products. But the chance that this study has any impact on your developing fetus is minuscule.

For starters, even the researchers (I interviewed one for an article) agreed that the study didn't allow them to say anything about humans because they hadn't studied humans. Another important point is that the researchers were reporting only on items made out of a class of plastics call polycarbonates. Most of what you eat and drink from isn't polycarbonates. If you feel more comfortable, though, use glass, ceramic, or metal containers to store food.

Should You Pump Gas?

Some of my patients have asked me about the signs they see posted at gas stations and near the entrances of certain buildings to warn that the product or place contains chemicals that may be dangerous to pregnant women. The legislation for these warnings differs from state to state (in California, it's called Proposition 65), and as you might expect, legislators pass these laws with good intentions: They want to protect and inform the population about biohazards and "dangerous" environmental toxins. Unfortunately, the law doesn't differentiate between the truly hazardous chemical refinery and the local gas pump (or your obstetrician's office, for that matter).

All of these businesses, by law, are supposed to post a warning to you that they have substances on the premises that may be a danger to pregnant women. In the case of your doctor's office, it's the bleach to clean instruments and the formaldehyde to preserve biopsies. In no way are these dangerous to you, yet the warning signs are the same.

The lesson here is not to fear these signs. In your routine daily life, you will not encounter nor be exposed to anything so dangerous to your little fetus. Once again, common sense on your part will make for a more relaxing pregnancy. So, please, go ahead and pump your own gas—and continue to see your OB!

In the Garden...

Always wear gloves when you're digging in the dirt. Outdoor cats poop everywhere, and there could always be cats other than yours leaving deposits in your yard.

FEAR: I won't be able to clean my bathroom.

FEARLESS FACT: You won't want to clean your bathroom (just kidding).

The real Fearless Fact is that super-strong cleaners may irritate your eyes, skin, or lungs, but they won't harm the baby. Unless, of course, you swallow them. So keep them out of your mouth, okay?

If you do find the smells irritating, there are a few simple solutions to the problem. One, avoid extra-strength cleaners and opt for mild ones such as unscented, general-purpose soaps and detergents, or try homemade cleaners such as baking soda and club soda. Two, get someone else to clean! As the mother of my good friend Mary once told me, "There's no special place in heaven for you just because you clean your own toilet."

I broke down near the last month of my pregnancy and hired someone to do my dirty work. She's still coming twice a month, and I have no plan to have her stop, ever. Once you have the baby, you'll see why any help like this is a godsend. I also had a friend who conned her younger sister into cleaning her bathroom for her while she was pregnant. Remember, when it comes to cleaning, it's not illegal to play on people's ignorance or sympathy. Of course, there may be paybacks. I'm waiting for the little sis to get pregnant; I don't see how my friend is going to get out of reciprocating.

Discount Cleaning Services

Don't throw those coupon mailers immediately into your recycling bin. Many cleaning companies send offers of discounts for expectant or new moms. If you don't find a coupon, call and ask.

Should You Paint the Nursery?

FEARLESS DOC

At least weekly I have patients ask me about fumes from common household products or paint. Many women want to paint the nursery. Is this safe? A good rule of thumb is, if the fumes don't bother you, they won't bother your unborn baby. Your body is a great filter that protects your baby well. If, however, the smell makes you nauseated or gives you a headache, then stay away.

Should You Rock Out?

FEARLESS DOC

Many women report feeling lots of fetal movement when there's loud, sustained noise such as what you hear at a sporting event or concert. There is no good data to suggest that exposure to this level of noise causes any permanent damage to a fetus. The increased movement most likely represents the baby's sensation of vibration, which keeps him or her awake. The baby isn't in distress, but you may be. It's not so comfortable to get kicked in the ribs! This is another one of those activities where you must decide for yourself whether the benefit of that once-in-a-lifetime concert or championship game outweighs any discomfort.

Stress and Pregnancy

FEAR: I'm under a lot of stress; this can't be good for the baby.

FEARLESS FACT: Stress isn't ideal for you, but your baby will shrug it off.

Being slammed by a family tragedy, work problems, or other stresses when you're pregnant isn't fair, but it happens. The only thing that might make you feel better is knowing that your baby will be born as healthy as ever despite what you're experiencing.

My friend Amy lost both of her parents a month before her due date. On top of this, she had twin three-year-old boys. Yet, her third son arrived in the world every bit as healthy and happy as his brothers. It was hard on Amy, but the extreme shock and grief she suffered didn't in any way send her into labor early or cause pregnancy or delivery problems.

I have had friends, however, who were under intense stress at work and felt that it was taking a physical toll on them. One said she started having contractions a couple of months before she was due because of extreme pressure from one of her clients. Stress can, indeed, cause an increased release of adrenaline, more gastrointestinal upsets, and loss of sleep. All of these elements can conceivably cause uterine irritability, which may lead to Braxton Hicks contractions and, eventually, to pre-term labor. But this situation can be easily handled (see The Lowdown on Braxton Hicks) and will almost never reach the point at which you actually go into pre-term labor. Of course, you don't want to have to handle this kind of problem if you don't have to.

My friend's solution was to dump her demanding client. She did this more for her own happiness than for the health of the baby, and, yes, she was noticeably happier afterwards. So if you want to quit something, blame the pregnancy if you like. Few people realize how invulnerable your baby really is, and they'll completely buy the excuse. Also, keep in mind that sometimes being pregnant gives you a new perspective on your life. If the cause of your stress is usually minor work issues or other such nuisances, you may be happy to find that they don't seem so important when you have a child growing inside.

Stress? What Stress?

FEARLESS Midwife

I'm a little cynical about stress. I always think that people in our culture overdramatize it. Just think, there are women living in war-torn countries who are practically starving and have the threat of death looming over their heads, and they still manage to reproduce. Of course, avoiding stress in general is a good idea, even when that stress is traffic and the fact that you have to wait in line at the dry cleaners.

The Lowdown on Braxton Hicks

Think of Braxton Hicks contractions as your uterus's rehearsal for the big day. From around the twentieth week on, many women have them. And most women who have a couple of kids have tons of Braxton Hicks, particularly around thirty-two weeks and after.

Don't worry. The contractions aren't strong enough to deliver the baby. They may be uncomfortable, however. If you have more than four in one hour, get off your feet and drink water. If the contractions last for a second hour and continue to be that frequent, it's probably still okay, but you should call your doctor or midwife. And you should definitely not make any more trips to Disneyland or go on exhausting, day-long shopping trips to the mall. Braxton Hicks are often your body's way of telling you to rest more.

The Stress Factor

FEARLESS DOC

I don't believe, nor is there any evidence to suggest, that stress can cause a normal pregnancy to miscarry or end in stillbirth. Stress can sometimes alter ovulation and make conception more difficult, but stress itself doesn't directly endanger an otherwise healthy pregnancy. Remember, the day-to-day human burdens that we interpret as stress have always been here; they were here for our ancestors as well. For example, living through the Great Depression probably wasn't easy. Yet, somehow, people did it, and we are all here as living proof that they did.

Sometimes, though, how we choose to deal with stress is a problem. Severe stress often disrupts our usual support systems and coping mechanisms. This may mean some women are more likely to eat poorly, drink alcohol, or abuse substances, all of which can certainly affect a developing fetus. For these women, there is a definite need for supportive intervention. With proper communication, therapy, and medication, if necessary, a happy outcome can still result.

Get a Healthy Handle on Stress

FEARLESS Midwife

How we cope with stress is partially inherited and partially learned. It makes sense that if you don't deal with stress in a healthy way, you're more likely to end up with children who handle it the same ineffective way. Becoming pregnant is a great time to reevaluate behavior and coping mechanisms and explore ways to set better examples for your babies to come. If you're feeling stressed, try exercising, talking to someone about your stress, or even writing about it in a journal.

Pets

FEARLESS DOC

Petting the family dog or cat is a great stress reducer. In fact, studies have shown that being around pets lowers blood pressure. But is it safe for pregnant women? Yes; almost all domesticated pets are safe for you and your newborn baby. In more than twenty years of practice, I have yet to see someone's pregnancy affected by her pet.

It's true there are reported diseases, called toxoplasmosis and psittacosis, that can be carried by cats or birds and may, in rare circumstances, threaten a pregnancy. If your cat is an indoor cat and is never exposed to feral cats, however, you have nothing to worry about. You can even go ahead and change the litter box. If your cat has access to the outdoors and there's any question in your mind, or if you just want to be extra safe, ask your partner to take care of this chore. Or you can wear gloves and a mask. There are also blood tests that can be ordered to determine your immunity or susceptibility to toxoplasmosis. Ask your practitioner if they are necessary in your situation.

If you have any concerns regarding the health of your bird as it relates to your pregnancy, consult your veterinarian. He or she should be able to perform an exam and any necessary tests to reassure you. There are no legitimate health concerns with dogs, horses, or household mammals or reptiles.

When Surgery Is Needed

There are rare occasions in pregnancy where surgery requiring anesthesia is necessary. Appendicitis, gall bladder disease, or trauma from an accident are but a few of the reasons. If surgery is deemed necessary by your doctor you can be sure that your baby's well being is being considered. These decisions are not taken lightly and the benefits of the surgery will outweigh any small risk. Of course, if surgery can be put off until the second trimester, of after delivery, it will be. And, should you need surgery, when possible, regional anesthesia, such as a spinal or epidural, is preferable. Sometimes a general anesthetic is required, though. You should feel quite comfortable knowing that even if you are put to sleep it will not harm your baby. Modern anesthetic medications make this much safer than you may have read in other sources.

When my friend Andie was five months pregnant with her second baby she had to have her gall bladder removed. The surgery was laproscopic but she did have to be knocked out completely. Of course, she fretted about the decision. But the truth is it was necessary. She could've been jeopardizing her health—and by extension the health of her unborn baby—if she would've refused it. The surgery went well and she recovered fine. What reassured Andie the most (besides being well-informed that the risk to her baby was minimal) was that her OB/GYN visited and checked her both pre-operatively and post-operatively. Furthermore, Andie had an ultrasound soon after the surgery. The ultrasound was solely to reassure her that the baby was fine—and it worked.

Going Places, and Not

FEAR: We'll have to cancel our plans to fly to a relative's wedding.

FEARLESS FACT: Air travel is generally safe throughout most of your pregnancy.

It sometimes *seems* as if everyone should just stay home and wait for your big day, but life goes on, of course, even though you're pregnant. That means other people get married, families want to take vacations, and even business trips pop up. Of course, some of this means you must get on an airplane. The good news: Air travel is safe for most pregnant women until almost the bitter end (the American College of Obstetrics and Gynecology, or ACOG, says thirty-six weeks). In the absence of complications, pregnant women can observe the same basic precautions for air travel as the general population. Now doesn't that make you feel like getting away? Here are additional ACOG tips for pregnant air travelers:

- To avoid blood clots (a concern for all travelers, pregnant or not), periodically move your lower legs to allow for proper blood circulation.
- To ease in-flight discomfort, pregnant women should avoid gaseous foods and drinks before flying.
- To avoid getting thrown about in the event of air turbulence, always use your seat belt.

Will the Airlines Allow You to Go?

Most U.S. airlines allow pregnant women to fly up to thirty-six weeks gestation on domestic flights. For international flights, thirty-five weeks is usually the limit. Many cruise lines have their own guidelines. Of course, nobody will be able to accurately tell how pregnant you are, so you can travel right up to the end if you want. But for comfort's sake (not to mention the possibility that you could deliver early), it's unlikely you'll want to travel much in the last six weeks or so.

When Not to Travel

Travel isn't recommended for pregnant women who have either medical or obstetric complications (for example, pregnancy-induced hypertension, poorly controlled diabetes, heart conditions, or sickle cell disease). The main reason is that you may need immediate medical attention, and you're not going to get it if you're cruising in the Bahamas or flying over Missouri. If you have any doubts, ask your doctor or midwife before you go.

Travel: Ask Yourself the Right Questions

FEARLESS Midwife

Generally, I recommend not traveling after thirty-six weeks, because delivery may occur at any time. Occasionally, though, I have women who insist on going to a wedding or some other major event. I always ask, "What will happen if you go into labor while you are there? How will you handle the postpartum time and getting back home?"

Although a local hospital may be available and no medical harm would come to mother or baby, many women find the thought of delivering in an unfamiliar location unsettling. There is also the issue of getting you back home after the delivery. A one-hour drive isn't a big deal, but a twelve-hour drive with a newborn after having a cesarean section is another thing.

Frequently, after we discuss the proposed trip, these women decide that they would rather stay home. If they don't, I always give them a copy of their records to take along and ask them to make a plan for how they will handle any emergencies.

One of the lessons we all learn as parents is that sometimes we have to change our plans when our children need us. Sometimes we have to miss a funeral, a wedding, or a great vacation because our child has the chicken pox or just had an emergency appendectomy. Before you have children, it's harder to understand that sometimes you have to turn down plans to go somewhere because of your pregnancy. But you need to remember that, as a pregnant woman, you have a child who might need you; it's just that the child is inside your body.

On Roughing It...

Before I knew I was pregnant, I signed up for a backpacking and climbing trip that was to take place when I was around seven months pregnant. Up until the time I was five months or so along, I was thinking, "Why not go? I don't have to do anything dangerous." As the time got closer, though, I thought, "Hmmm..., maybe not." I ended up not going because I didn't want to deal with being any more hot, tired, or uncomfortable than I needed to be. Plus, all pregnant women go to the bathroom often, and I didn't want to deal with that in the great outdoors.

My friend Kathryn, who traveled often during her pregnancy, went on a cabin camping trip with her family a couple of months away from giving birth. She cut the trip short and headed home because she was miserable. The lesson: You may love the idea of roughing it at all other times in your life, but when you're extremely pregnant, being home with your comfy bed, convenient bathroom, and beckoning couch is really a good thing.

Travel Comfort and Discomfort

If you have had no problems in your pregnancy and you feel well, you may safely travel through most of your pregnancy. For pure comfort reasons, I always advise patients not to plan a vacation after thirty-two weeks. However, if you need to travel for business or a family event, it's generally safe to do so.

If you're flying, I suggest you sit in an aisle seat, walk around a bit, and, of course, keep your bladder empty. It's a good idea to wear loose-fitting shoes and avoid salty foods and drinks since they increase the tendency for your feet to swell. This isn't a medical problem necessarily, but it may be uncomfortable.

Your choice of destinations can also be a factor. It makes sense to avoid remote or exotic locations often lacking in good emergency medical care. Cleveland and Paris are all right, but I would recommend you put off backpacking in Nepal until a later date.

When Dad Wants to Go

I'm frequently asked if it's okay for the dad to travel near the due date. Assuming the woman would have a way to get to the hospital (friends or family), I always pose this question. "How would both of you feel if he missed the delivery? Who would take care of your other children?" Usually, couples decide that the dad should stay home. Often, these trips are not to attend major life events (funerals or weddings) but are fishing trips with brothers or other primarily recreational events. Again, this is a time when parents need to begin realizing that sometimes they must put their own desires behind the needs of their child and the pregnant partner.

~ *Fast and Fearless*

Here's what you need to know about travel and pregnancy:

- Travel is usually safe and permissible (up to at least thirty-five weeks), unless your doctor has told you not to travel.
- Less exotic locales are usually better at providing comfort, clean water and food, and access to medical facilities.
- If you fly, sit in an aisle seat. Also, avoid salty foods and wear loose shoes.

FEAR: Sleeping on my stomach will harm the baby.

FEARLESS FACT: Sleeping any way you can is better than not.

My sister-in-law always slept on her stomach, and once she became pregnant, she was terrified that it would do something to hurt the baby. Every time she woke up, though, she was on her stomach. If this is you, don't worry. There is some evidence that sleeping on your back or stomach can decrease blood flow to the baby, but the truth is pregnant women are rarely able to sleep on their stomachs or backs for long.

By the end of the first trimester, even my confirmed stomach-sleeper sister-in-law was no longer waking up on her belly. Instead, she was playing the pillow game—trying to find a way to prop up her belly or feet or whatever. Your increased girth not only makes it difficult to get out of bed (don't be surprised if your partner has to give you a push), but it makes it difficult to get comfortable. If you can catch a few z's on your stomach or back, do it. But you'll probably find yourself quickly shifting to another position.

Is Bed Rest "Really" Necessary?

FEARLESS Midwife

Statistically, about 25 percent of pregnant women are put on a week or more of bed rest in an effort to avoid complications and pre-term births (that means births prior to thirty-seven weeks). Lately, researchers have argued that bed rest has never been shown in studies to achieve its desired goals.

In my experience, though, it works. And because I realize how difficult it is for anyone, let alone a pregnant woman, to stay in bed, I prescribe bed rest only when absolutely necessary. My recommendation on this one is that if your practitioner feels you need it, hit the sack. I've had only positive results with it; and mark my words, after a month or two of taking care of a newborn, you'll wish somebody would put you on bed rest! Here are some tips for getting the most from your bed rest:

- Lie on your side and use pillows to support your abdomen, upper leg, shoulders, and back. Switch sides every hour or so.
- Make sure you have the telephone, remote control, and water nearby.
- Invite your other children and/or your pet to keep you company in bed.
- If friends, relatives, or neighbors offer to help, accept; if they don't, ask. This is also a good rule to follow when you have a newborn.

Sleep When You Can

FEARLESS Midwife

Whether you have insomnia or are just plain uncomfortable, it can be hard to sleep while you're pregnant. So if you can sleep, sleep! Whenever, wherever, however. Many pregnant women end up on the couch or in a recliner because it's the only place they can get comfortable.

Then again, you might want to think of this lack of sleep as training. Some people theorize it's conditioning you for the fewer hours of sleep you'll get with a newborn in the house.

~ *Fast and Fearless*

Here's what you need to know to live fearless and pregnant:

- What you ate, drank, or inhaled prior to knowing you were pregnant is likely of no consequence. Discuss it with your doctor, though, for reassurance.
- Unless you swallow them, few everyday cleaning products or cosmetics are known to be harmful to developing fetuses.
- Danger signs on gas pumps and medical buildings are out of line; your environment is unlikely to harm your baby or you.
- Have as much sex as you want, unless your doctor or midwife tells you not to.
- Stress and noise won't harm your baby, but they also do nothing for your comfort or happiness.

- Despite what you've heard, if your cat is an indoor pet not exposed to feral cats, you can change the litter box. Other pets pose no problems.
- Sleep in whatever position you can, and feel fortunate if you can sleep.
- Color your hair, clean your teeth, get your nails done, and have a massage, but skip the Retin-A and Botox.
- Unless your doctor says not to, it's safe to travel while pregnant up to thirty-five weeks or so. For comfort and the security of knowing you'll have your baby at home, however, you may not want to travel much after thirty-two weeks (ditto for your partner).
- Unless you're a super die-hard camper, forget about roughing it.

7

Fearless Gear Buying

"Baby gear? It's an industry that tries to make as much money as possible from parents and parents-to-be by using fear as the base tactic. Not that there are not real concerns a parent must consider, but just not all that's promoted."

– Livia, mother of two-year-old Jake with baby number two on the way

"My husband and I walked into the baby superstore and all we could think was, 'Oh my God! How will we ever figure this out?' It was enough to make us want to go home and lie down and just forget about it."

– Karen, sixteen weeks pregnant

"You look at all of the crap on the 'must-have' registry lists, and you think (as my husband so eloquently put it), 'All they really need is some diapers, a bed, and a pair of boobs.' But that's not true in reality. They do need a lot of stuff… And a lot of it just makes your life easier. Sure, they don't need a bouncy seat… just like you don't need a shower every day—but it sure is nice!"

– Jenna, mother of ten-month-old Sophie Bella

FEAR: I won't have the "right" gear.

FEARLESS FACT: There's amazingly little you really need in the first few months.

Baby productland is truly overwhelming for most novices. After one initial, dizzying foray into the baby warehouse superstore, my husband and I decided instead to register online for my shower. Mostly, we sat staring at the monitor saying, "Oh, now that looks cool, but do they make it in black?" What I'm saying is that we were using our old childless (I didn't say childish!) shopping habits. We were looking for sleek design, understated color, something that said, "Yes, I'm a parent, but I'm still with it, darn it!"

Occasionally, I'd read one of those online reviews that are supposedly written by real parents, and I tried to use sound judgment in deciding what we should buy. We also consulted our own secret weapon, my niece Jen, who had Sarah nine weeks before my son was born, spent hours in the stores, and researched the heck out of all conceivable items. Of course, we also tried to pay attention to what we saw other parents using and what other parents told us they liked. The result: We had some hits and misses, Jen had hits and misses, and every single parent will have hits and misses. But they won't be the same!

The truth is, there is no "right" baby gear. You can do your best to guess which features or products you might like, but you have no real way of telling what your baby is going to go for. Some babies like slings; some hate them. Some babies like their car seats, and some don't. Your child may cry every time he or she is plopped in a stroller that's extremely popular and looks comfy and then be delighted to land in a cheap umbrella stroller that doesn't have any padding.

Don't waste your pregnancy stressing over baby gear. Talk to a few moms who've had babies recently (gear changes fast) and then go to the store to handle bigger ticket items such as the car seat, stroller, play yard, and high chair. Remember, too, that most of this stuff and most of what you may get at your shower won't be used until several months down the road. You can wait to buy most items as you need or want them.

And don't forget about used stuff. Most parents are dying to pass along their babe's used clothing and outgrown gear. You might not have to buy—or get stressed about—as much stuff as you think. I also have to warn you, though, that once you get used to having the baby, you might even get addicted to the baby gear/toy store. It's no longer harrowing; it's fun!

> ***Not All Women Love to Shop***
>
> If you fear being overwhelmed when you walk into the cavernous baby superstore, check out the online stores first. You can browse at your leisure and read up on the products. Try:
>
> - Babycenter.com
> - Babiesrus.com

See also the section on Baby Gear Broken Down, *page 157.*

Does Used Equal Germs?

FEARLESS DOC

Some mothers worry that used clothes somehow mean used germs. That's not true at all. Just wash the clothes with detergent, and they'll be fine. Remember, all humans live in symbiosis with germs. That means we live in relative harmony with germs around us all the time—and your baby will too.

Gear: Fantasy Versus Reality

The ultimate baby gear irony is that most moms will admit that the least useful or least successful items turn out to be the splurges—those really cool things you may secretly imagine yourself having as you walk down the street. There you are, the stylish, slender (we're all immediately slender in our fantasies) mom, pushing a sleek, sporty, foreign-made stroller with a smiling baby decked out in the latest whatever. You know, what Sarah Jessica Parker's baby wore!

Remember, though, that there's no telling whether your baby will be as enamored as you are of whatever you've purchased. My son didn't like the stroller until much later. He didn't love the infant car seat, even though it had a debonair herringbone pattern. And he didn't wear the beautiful handmade wool cap and booties (what my husband and I referred to as "works of art" in our pre-baby days), because by the time it was chilly enough to wear them, they didn't fit right. For now, go ahead and fantasize. But don't be disappointed if it doesn't work out exactly as you envision.

From the Fearless Midwife:

Baby Gear Broken Down

If you're having anxiety over baby gear, try getting down to the basics. What do you really need for a baby, and when do you need it?

First Month

ABSOLUTE ESSENTIALS:

- Newborn diapers
- Dry wipes or wipes formulated for newborns
- Basic clothing (onesies and sleeping sacks, for example)
- Burp cloths (cloth diapers work well)
- Infant car seat/carrier
- A place for the baby to sleep (not necessarily a crib)
- Nursing bras and pads, or newborn bottles and formula
- A comprehensive baby care book (I recommend *The Baby Book* by Martha and William Sears)
- Thermometer (an ear thermometer is easiest to use)
- Diaper rash cream
- Nail file (often works better than a nail clipper for newborns)

HELPFUL BUT NOT ESSENTIALS:

- Changing table and pad
- Stroller
- Sling
- Bassinet
- Breast-feeding pillow (if breast-feeding, of course)
- Breast pump (if breast-feeding)
- Baby bathtub
- Monitor (if your baby will be sleeping out of earshot)

Second Month On

USEFUL, PERHAPS ESSENTIAL ITEMS:

- Bouncy seat
- Play yard
- Toys that vibrate, jiggle, or play music and, you hope, entertain your baby
- Overhead play structures like a Gymini

Sixth Month On

USEFUL, PERHAPS ESSENTIAL ITEMS:

- Umbrella stroller (light and easy to transport)
- High chair or seat that attaches to the kitchen table
- Car seat for a child greater than 20 pounds (some switch from rear-facing to front-facing; once your child weighs more than 40 pounds, you'll trade up to a booster seat that faces front)
- More diapers, wipes, clothes, toys, and *money!*

Bathing Your Baby after Delivery

Some moms don't buy baby bathtubs. Instead, they bathe their babies when they do. For the mother, a bath is fine from about one week after delivery on, whether you've had a vaginal birth or a c-section. But because babies have sensitive skin, some pediatricians recommend that you wait about a month (or, at the very least, until the cord has fallen off) before submerging a newborn in a bath. Until then, you usually give them sponge baths. Check with your pediatrician for his or her recommendation.

And, by the way, don't waste money on duckies or other items that tell you if the bath water is too hot. You have a highly sensitive device attached to your body that works just as well: your elbow. Poke your elbow in the water; if the temperature feels hot to the elbow, it's too hot for the baby.

Listen to Other Moms

Talk to other moms before you buy a ton of gear—lots of moms. It always seems to me that the more children a woman has, the less stuff she hauls around. I think they're onto something.

Other moms can give you lots of input on what they like and why. Also, remember that many things look great, but some babies hate them and are never happy with them. My own baby hated her $300 stroller but was quite content in a $20 umbrella-style stroller. I sold her crib when she was one year old because she'd never slept in it. When possible, borrow gear from a friend at least long enough to experiment on your baby to see if she likes the stuff.

Most Important, Listen to Yourself!

I sent an email out to several of my mom-friends asking which gear they loved and what they thought was worthless, unsafe, etc. The first email I got back was from Anne, who told me the only thing that came to mind was a walker (you're generally in the market for something like this at around six months). Anne said she instantly felt that walkers weren't safe *at all* and then later heard that, indeed, they were hazardous. Instead, you should buy a stationary exersaucer. I laughed out loud because just two days earlier I'd made a special trip just to buy my son a walker! And he loved being able to move on his own!

Our house is a one-level, open floor plan and has hardwood floors, no drapery cords, and no china cabinets or bric-a-brac that he could grab or have fall on him. I moved a few items, and we plugged up the outlets, naturally, but overall my husband and I deemed the walker safe. Of course, we still kept an eye on him. The lesson in this is that, sure, you can talk to your friends, but in the end you have to take a close look at your particular circumstances and make your own decisions. That's true for baby gear and just about everything in motherhood.

On Breast Pumps…

I attended a three-hour, hospital-sponsored breast-feeding class and was told by the instructor that a certain pump was great and available at the hospital for around $100. I bought one, marked it off my list, and put it on the shelf. Of course, two months later when I had the baby and needed it, I was fumbling around with tubes and funnels and panicking.

Fortunately, although pumps look daunting, most are not hard to figure out. The thing was, the pump I had was electric (which is good), but it was the sort where you had to move your thumb on and off of a small hole to make it work. Even though I knew nothing of pumps, this didn't seem like a good design.

Lo and behold, when I finally spoke with a lactation consultant, I was informed what I bought was a waste. She told me I needed a hospital-grade electric pump, which, of course, I could rent from her. The rental for six months was about what you'd pay for a good (but not hospital-grade) pump. My rented pump was nearly the size of a toaster oven, but it was extremely quiet and, best of all, actually worked.

On the Great Stroller Dilemma

Selecting a stroller is daunting. Most people believe they have to make a choice between a huge SUV of a stroller with the infant carrier seat that clicks into it (called a "stroller system") or a regular stroller that may be lighter and easier to use but doesn't offer the convenience of the infant carrier seat. Not true! You can have it both ways. There's something called a Snap-N-Go that's great—lightweight, super easy to use, and compatible with all infant seats. It's just a frame on wheels that the carrier seat hooks into.

When your child reaches around twenty pounds, he or she will be done with the infant carrier seat and will graduate to a car seat for heavier kids, which will remain in your car nearly all the time. Then you can choose a stroller that works best for you. Don't be surprised if it's not the hot model; many kids and moms love the cheap and easy-to-use umbrella strollers.

FEAR: I won't be able to put all this gear together.

FEARLESS FACT: Much of today's baby gear comes pre-assembled or partially assembled.

I was absolutely overwhelmed with all the baby gear—even things like bottles and sterilizers had instructions. I remember my friend Donna telling me that just learning how to use the gear would give me a sense of confidence. If you're like me, you won't feel as if your postpartum gray matter is flexible enough to really learn anything. But Donna turned out to be right. I muddled through and even mastered a few things and so will you.

It can be daunting to assemble everything. If you have a friend or family member who is generally good at this stuff, ask for help! Also, know that baby gear is going the way of computers; lots of it comes almost out-of-the-box ready. Manufacturers must realize that new parents have a lot on their minds and can't deal with tricky IKEA-style assembly directions. Thank goodness. I've noticed, too, that some manufacturers are putting big bold notices in the boxes saying, "If you have a problem with assembly, call 1-800-xxxx. Don't take this back to the store." So just breathe. Get the stuff out of the box. You'll be pleasantly surprised to find much of it is pre-assembled. Know that, yes, you can do this. And if you can't, call the 800 number.

Battery Torture

FYI: Lots of baby items take batteries (usually AA, C, or D). Get a bunch and have them on hand for that fateful day when the bouncy seat could be your savior if only twinkle-twinkle didn't sound like wahhh-wah-wah. Also imperative: a Phillips head screwdriver. The battery panel is always screwed on. This makes changing the batteries more of a pain, but at least you'll never find your tyke sucking on a D-cell.

What Not to Buy

FEARLESS DOC

Shopping for pregnancy, labor, and the newborn can be a tremendous joy as you plan for your new life. And, of course, in a free country we can spend our hard-earned money any way we please. There are, however, a few things that may tempt you but that you might want to resist placing on your baby shower registry or in your shopping cart.

1. Resist any books or videos that describe what to expect during these times but that instill fear rather than confidence. I've spoken to many patients and colleagues about these instructional aids, and most find them more frightening than helpful. This, as much as anything else, helped motivate me to co-write this book.
2. Pass up Doppler devices to listen to your unborn baby. Hearing the baby's heartbeat never fails to bring a smile to the face of an expecting mother. It makes those prenatal visits a bit more exciting. The Doppler device your practitioner uses, however, costs about $900. Please do not run out and purchase this or a cheaper version at Toys R Us. Not only is it an unnecessary expense, but if your partner or you listen and can't find the heartbeat, it will create anxiety of major proportions.
3. Don't buy apnea monitors for newborns unless prescribed by your pediatrician. This device is supposed to warn you when your baby stops breathing, but it gives so many false alarms that you will either go crazy or just turn it off.

Other Items to Leave on the Shelf

Most mothers tell you that bottle warmers, wipe warmers, and foam devices that prevent the baby from rolling and having "flat head syndrome" are fairly useless. You can't take these in your carry bag, and they will most likely end up on a shelf. I found the wipe warmer a great idea in concept but ridiculous in practice. By the time I got the wipe out and on my baby's rear, it was cold again. Besides, halfway through the stack, the warmer dried out the wipes. The third time I went for a wipe and found a dried-out, brownish, crackly thing instead, I unplugged the warmer and threw it in the garage.

The foam device to prevent rolling/flat head syndrome also looked good but turned out to be useless. Babies can't roll for several months, and by the time they're able to roll, it's fine to allow them to do so in their safe sleeping space (usually a crib or co-sleeper). The best way to prevent "flat head syndrome" is to make sure you turn your baby's head to alternating sides when you put him or her down to sleep. If you have a serious flat-head problem, your pediatrician will recommend other ways to solve it.

Olfactophobia and the Genie Thing

Something most new parents anticipate fearing is the smell of dirty diapers. Special receptacles (like one called the Diaper Genie) have become very popular. Most take specific liners, and some are a real chore to change. If you truly are olfactophobic (fear smells), you will really hate changing these liners. Why? With the special receptacles, you often end up emptying them much less often (like once a week). Also, the receptacles are made of plastic, and it doesn't take long for the smell to somehow permeate the container.

I found a better solution to be a small wastebasket with a swinging lid, which made diaper depositing easy. I emptied this once or twice a day and used plastic grocery store bags as liners.

"All of us are born with a set of instinctive fears—of falling, of the dark, of lobsters, of falling on lobsters in the dark or speaking before a Rotary Club, and of the words 'Some Assembly Required.'"

– Dave Barry

Do You Need to Sterilize Bottles?

It used to be, according to my mother-in-law, that glass bottles were boiled on the stove, and all kinds of care was taken to sterilize them. If you're using bottles, you'll likely flip out in the first few months and try to sterilize them. You might buy the electric sterilizer or the microwave steamer/sterilizers. They're not expensive, and they're easy to use, but they aren't necessary.

You can wash baby bottles as you wash your own dishes, with hot water and dish soap or in the dishwasher (put the bottles and nipples in the top rack). That's sterile enough even for a newborn. If you don't want to constantly wash bottles, try using the bottles with the drop-in disposable liners. That way you only have to worry about the nipples.

FEAR: I just found out my infant car seat isn't A-rated.

FEARLESS FACT: The rating system isn't specifically grading the seat's safety.

The National Highway Traffic Safety Administration (NHTSA) rates car seats for infants and older children, but the system, interestingly enough, is something called an "ease of use" rating. It doesn't compare the performance of different child restraints in the event of a crash. The point, though, is that a child restraint is most effective if it is correctly installed in a vehicle and if the child is correctly secured in the restraint. A child restraint that is easier to use should have a lower rate of misuse. Therefore, the rating system isn't worthless; it just indirectly relates to safety.

For now, all we can assume is that all the car seats allowed to be on the market are equally safe but, perhaps, aren't equally easy to use. I'm not sure how easy it is to use any of them. Although my husband claims anyone can install these seats and says they're not that difficult, a recent NHTSA survey found that more than 70 percent of all child car seats were being used improperly. Infant car seats are secured in your car with existing seat belts and/or supplemental belts. If you hate reading instructions and monkeying around with this stuff, you can hire someone to install it for you or to double check your installation. Go to the NHTSA web site (www.nhtsa.com) to locate someone in your area.

What Does NHTSA Rate?

Under the NHTSA rating system, car seats are given an overall ease-of-use rating at the "A," "B," or "C" level. The overall rating is determined based on the letter grades the seat receives in each of the following five categories:

- Whether the restraint is pre-assembled or requires assembly after purchase
- Whether the labeling attached to the restraint is clear
- Whether the written instructions are clear in explaining the restraint's proper use
- How easy it is to secure a child correctly in the restraint
- Whether the seat has features that make it easier to install in a vehicle

You can go on the NHTSA web site and look at a whole variety of car seats and their ease-of-use ratings, but what I found is that the kinks perhaps need to be worked out of this rating system. There were car seats that received a "C" in one category and "A's" in the rest and then earned an overall grade of "B." Then there were other seats that had four "A's" and one "C" but got an overall grade of "A."

There's hope, though, that we'll have a better rating system by your next pregnancy. NHTSA is conducting a pilot test of simulated crashes to determine how well child restraints perform and how well certain vehicles protect children. At the conclusion of the pilot program, the NHTSA will decide whether to do further testing and/or compile this information for consumers.

Q & A with a Car Seat Expert

We asked Lori Jacobs, a certified child passenger safety technician based in Thousand Oaks, California, to answer the following questions:

1. Can we assume that all car seats on the market are equally safe as long as they're installed properly?

All car seats on the market must meet the same federal standards, but there are some differences. In particular, five-point harnesses are considered by experts to be a better choice than other harness styles.

2. Does the price of the car seat influence the safety of the car seat (that is, does more expensive equal safer)?

Generally not. In some cases, a less expensive seat is sold with a fancy cover, often leather or suede or with a recognized designer name. There are no additional features, yet the price goes up by more than double.

However, there are some products for which more expensive means more convenience features. Such a seat is not really safer than a less expensive product if both are used correctly, but because it is easier to use correctly, it is more likely that it will be on a regular basis. An example would be harness adjusters—some are easy to access and use daily, others much more difficult. It is important that the harness be adjusted regularly to fit the child, not just for growth, but for changes in clothing. A child in a sweatsuit on a chilly morning needs a different harness adjustment than the same child in a tee-shirt and shorts in the afternoon. I sometimes call this the "cuss factor"—the more you will want to cuss at the seat during use, the less likely you will be to follow through on correct use every time.

3. What should parents look for in a seat?

First, check to be sure it fits your vehicle securely. There are frequently compatibility issues between the child restraint and the vehicle, and finding the one that fits your car is important. The new LATCH system is expected to reduce these problems, but not all parents have the newer LATCH-equipped vehicles, and since the LATCH system is fairly new, a few compatibility "bugs" are still being worked on.

Second, make sure it is the correct restraint for your child's age and weight. Most infants fit better in infant-only seats, but if you prefer to use a convertible seat from birth, choose one with a low set of harness strap slots (most models have three choices, but their actual measurements vary) and two or more crotch strap positions to fit a newborn to a preschooler.

Children should remain in a harness as long as possible, at least to forty pounds. Some children are ready for a belt-positioning booster at forty pounds, but others need a harness longer. There are a few choices on the market right now that can be used to a higher weight, and they have the harness. It is hoped that this trend will continue. As a general guideline, a child is rarely ready for a booster before age four, though a few bigger, mature children will sit properly in one at age three. If your child reaches forty pounds before this age or before you think he is mature enough to use a booster, look for a harnessed seat with a higher weight limit.

Finally, consider the convenience of use of the product. Experiment with the harness adjuster; is it easy to access and use once the restraint is installed in your vehicle? If the seat can be used as both rear- and forward-facing, try it both ways so you don't end up disappointed when you change modes. Choose the model that installs in your vehicle securely without the need for heroic measures. If you need a 200-pound firefighter to struggle to install the seat at an official installation site, remember that you won't be able to bring him home with you when you need to move the seat to Grandma's car next week. Check the tether strap adjuster on convertible or forward-facing seats as well; some are more difficult to adjust than others.

4. Do you have any general tips on installation?

If it isn't tight, it isn't right. There's no such thing as "good enough" in car seat installation; you have to achieve a snug fit in the vehicle in order to protect the child. If you can't, then seek help.

Also, I like to tell parents that creativity will be a very useful trait in parenting—you will use it in art, play, education, and discipline. However, there is *no creativity allowed* in child restraints. Read the restraint's instruction manual and the vehicle manual, educate yourself, stick to the recommended methods, and seek trained, expert help with installation if you really need it.

For more information on car seats, contact this non-profit organization dedicated to public education and advocacy:

SafetyBeltSafe USA
www.carseat.org • Phone 800-222-6860

Car Seat Basics

- Infants from birth to the age of one should ride in the back seat in a rear-facing safety seat. Once your child hits a year (and weighs twenty pounds or more), he or she can ride in the back seat in a forward-facing safety seat.
- Harness straps should fit snugly and be at or below your baby's shoulders.
- The harness chest clip should be placed at the infant's armpit level. This keeps the harness straps positioned properly.

FEAR: I bought a used crib, and now I've heard used cribs aren't safe.

FEARLESS FACT: Used cribs are generally fine.

My friend Jenna got a really cute used crib that went great with her rustic-chic décor. Then she made the mistake of reading some well-meaning (I'm sure) baby gear book that claimed a used mattress could contribute to SIDS. She was at her pinnacle of pregnantness, and yet she dragged the mattress to the curb and called her husband in a panic to meet her at Sears to buy a new one. Of course, that's just what they did. But the truth is they didn't have to. The U.S. Consumer Product Safety Commission says that used cribs and mattresses are completely safe as long as they meet the following standards:

- The mattress is firm and tight-fitting: This makes changing the sheet a royal pain, but it ensures the baby doesn't get wedged between the mattress and crib.
- There are no loose, missing, or broken slats or hardware: You surely wouldn't want the whole thing to fall apart. Also, check that any parts that are glued together are secure.
- There is no more than the width of a soda can between crib slats: That's two and three-eighths inches for those of you with a ruler. Wider than this and there's a risk the baby could stick his or her little head through.
- The corner posts aren't over one-sixteenth of an inch high: Short corner posts or no posts ensure the baby's clothes won't get caught on them.
- There are no cutout designs in the headboard or footboard: Again, you don't want your baby sticking his or her head through anything.

Sleeping Together

One of the most controversial issues in parenting (just behind breast versus bottle) is where your baby sleeps. Many parents love to have their baby sleep in its own crib, and the baby does quite nicely there. Other parents have their babies sleep with them. The American Academy of Pediatrics currently recommends against having your baby sleep with you because there may be an increased risk of suffocation. If you do this anyway, please follow these tips for bed-sharing:

- Don't allow older siblings to sleep with a baby under nine months. Sleeping children won't have the same awareness that you have.
- Place the baby next to you, rather than between you and your partner. Mothers seem to be physically and mentally aware instantly of their baby's presence, so it's extremely unlikely they will roll over on their babies. After a few months of bed-sharing, dads will also develop this keen awareness.
- Your baby should always be placed on its back to sleep (no matter where that may be).
- Avoid cushiony couches, waterbeds, or any "sinky" surfaces that could pose a suffocation risk.
- Don't bundle your babe; your warm body is an added heat source. Also, avoid strong hair sprays, deodorants, and perfumes; they may irritate and clog your baby's nasal passages.
- Skip dangling jewelry, lingerie with string ties, and anything your baby could get tangled up in. (You probably won't be wearing this kind of stuff for a while anyhow.)
- A bigger bed is better than a smaller one. If you can, trade your double for a comfy queen or king size.
- Consider a co-sleeper. Some parents (and babies) sleep better if the baby is within touching and hearing distance, but not in the same bed. In this case, a bedside co-sleeper is a good option.

FIVE REASONS NOT TO SLEEP TOGETHER

Never sleep with the baby if:

1. You've drunk alcohol or taken medication or illicit drugs. If you're tipsy in any way (even some cold medicines can have this effect), you won't be as sensitive to your baby, and you may not wake as easily.
2. You're morbidly obese. There's more of a smothering risk, and obesity has been linked with sleep disorders that could interfere with your alertness.
3. You're extremely exhausted from sleep deprivation. Exhaustion can work the same as drugs, lessening your sensitivity to the baby and causing you not to wake quickly.
4. You're on a very cushiony surface, such as a waterbed or couch.
5. You're the child's babysitter. A sitter's innate awareness and sensitivity to the baby isn't usually as acute as a mom's.

By the way, new doesn't mean problem free. New cribs sometimes get recalled for defects, like slats falling out too easily. For instance, even though no injuries were sustained, one new crib was recalled because twelve people across the U.S. reported that one or several slats on the drop side of the crib detached. There are even examples of baby products being recalled after only one complaint and no injuries.

If you're someone who doesn't like the government to dictate your life, or if you think all this sounds a bit reactionary, you might not see recalls and safety regulations as a positive thing. On the other hand, it's reassuring for many parents that manufacturers of baby gear are safety sensitive (with, of course, the encouragement of our government) and voluntarily recall their products so readily.

Register Your Baby Gear

Most major baby items come with registration cards. You can usually register by mail or online. I normally hate dealing with this sort of busy work, but with major baby gear, it's a good idea. If anything you have is recalled, the manufacturer will contact you and give you instructions on how to get the item replaced. You can also log on to the Consumer Product Safety Commission web site at http://CPSC.gov to see if a product has been recalled.

FEAR: My baby will fall out of the sling.

FEARLESS FACT: Various types of slings have been used since time began (or around that date).

Slings are just a piece of fabric that hangs over you from one shoulder to the opposite hip and makes a hammock for the baby. Most of them also allow different configurations, such as a front carrier, backpack, or hip sling. When you have a little seven-pound human you've worked hard to bring into this world, it's natural to feel a bit nervous about placing your infant inside this fabric and trusting that he or she won't fall out or the shoulder clip won't give. You have to remember, however, that mothers in cultures worldwide were using various slings and packs to carry their young long, long before the stroller was invented. Many of these mothers ran through wild jungles, whereas you're only going to the grocery store.

In short, slings are perfectly safe. The only thing you really have to remember is that you need to have fabric on both sides of the child, and you need to have the sling cinched correctly (take a look at the directions). Also, sit down the first few times you put your baby in or lift your baby out. Once you get the hang of it, you'll toss your little one into the sling, answer the phone, and feed the dog all at the same time.

Carrying Your Baby after Delivery

Whether you've had a vaginal delivery or a cesarean section, using a sling or any kind of carrying device is perfectly fine—as long as your baby weighs in under twenty pounds (and let's hope he or she does).

FEAR: I'm a bad mother if I put my baby in a play pen.

FEARLESS FACT: It's often wiser and safer for the baby to be contained.

My friend Kathryn, who is the consummate organic-food-eating earth mother, fretted nonstop about this. We've all heard how play pens are basically baby jails (that's my husband's term) that neglectful parents use. But that was yesteryear. Today, they are *not* called play pens. They've been renamed play yards, which makes all the difference (well, some anyway).

Kathryn's husband Jon convinced her, though, that a play yard was much safer for the baby whenever she had to take her eyes off of him to, say, answer the door or check her E-mail. I totally agree. Nobody should leave a baby for hours in a play anything, although I have a tough time envisioning this could even happen. I know my own son would complain so loudly that anyone would give in and take him out. Even so, it's fine to find a safe and comfortable place for the baby while you take care of some minor business. It's not neglectful or "bad." It's called being responsible.

~ *Fast and Fearless*

Here's all you need to know about baby gear:

- Don't worry about buying the right gear. Your baby will like some items and not like others. There's no way for you to tell before you try them.
- There isn't a lot you need in the first month, so don't sweat it too much. What you definitely need are diapers, wipes, onesies, sleepers, a bassinet or crib (unless the baby will sleep with you), and bottles and formula or nursing bras and pads.
- Consider registering for most of your shower items online. You can read about products at your leisure and compare features. Sites with plenty of gear and information include babycenter.com or babiesrus.com.
- What you think is cool and *très* mommy chic is probably the item your baby won't like. Don't be too disappointed—the fantasy was fun while it lasted.
- Yes, if you want to, you can sleep with your baby. Take the proper precautions, but don't be ashamed about it.
- Don't buy a second-rate breast pump. In fact, consider renting a hospital-grade one from a lactation shop or consultant when (or if) you need it.
- For strollers, make the trip to the store. Test-pushing is the best way to select the one that suits you.
- Since no official rating exists yet, all car seats are created equal in safety. Some, however, are more difficult than others to install and use properly. Get help with installation if you need it.
- Used stuff in good shape is just fine.

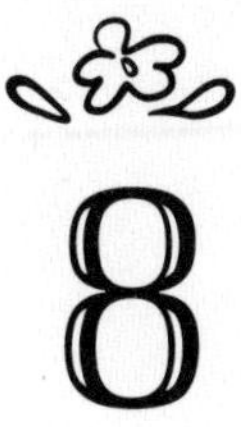

8

Fearless Delivery Prep

"As the birth grows closer, I'm finding myself sometimes really nervous but also with a feeling of surrendering to the process, because I know that the only way to help myself deal is to remain calm and stay focused… Birth is going to happen as it happens."

– from the pregnancy journal of Hadley, mother of four-year-old Emory and seven-month-old Jasper

"The thought of pushing a baby out 'down there' was scary. Therefore, when I chose my OB, I made sure that he supported the use of epidurals and other pain management medications. As my pregnancy progressed, though, I began to appreciate the amazing work my body was doing. About two months before my due date, I informed my doctor that I wanted to try and have a natural, unmedicated birth. He was very supportive and encouraging. It ended up being an amazing, empowering experience."

– Dorothy, mother of six-month-old Edison

Sooner than you think, you'll find yourself in the third trimester. All those concerns that never materialized during the first two trimesters are now in the past. Your baby is almost ready for life outside the uterus, and a whole new series of questions begins to enter your mind. Preparing for labor and the delivery of your baby may seem frightening and a bit overwhelming, but there are few thoughts more reassuring than this: all babies are born, most without incident. You will not be in labor forever. With knowledge of what to expect comes peace of mind.

At your prenatal visits you should be discussing the preparations for labor and delivery with your doctor or midwife. Write down any questions you have so you can remember them at your visit. Forgetfulness is a common occurrence in the latter weeks of pregnancy. You have a lot on your mind.

Perineum Exercises

As we discussed in chapter 4, you may want to start massaging your perineum about a month away from your due date. This area, which lies between your vagina and anus, needs to stretch as the baby is delivered. Massage the area gently by placing your thumb in your vagina and gently pushing toward your anus while moving slowly back and forth. A lubricant like K-Y Jelly helps, as does moisturizing the external skin of the perineum with vitamin E oil to increase elasticity.

FEAR: I won't take the right childbirth class.

FEARLESS FACT: You'll have your baby even if you take no class.

Childbirth educators must be applauded. It was the Lamaze people, in fact, who revolutionized how most of us have babies. Not so long ago, women were knocked out, and the fathers were left pacing the waiting room. Nowadays, though, the pendulum has swung the other way. It's almost mandatory (or at least most of us feel that way) to be educated and proactive in the birth experience. That usually means some sort of childbirth education class is in store.

Some of the classes out there are based on one philosophy. The Lamaze or Bradley methods, for instance, have their own breathing and relaxation techniques and are intended to help you have your baby without pain medication. If you're vehemently opposed to the possibility of having pain medication, it's great to explore these or other similar philosophies. But know too that you can't go wrong with any class you take.

I called to enroll in a birthing class when I was just under three months from my due date. I thought this was plenty of time and was shocked when the reception I got was sort of like I'd called the Ritz-Carlton and asked to book my wedding on the second Saturday in June. So my husband and I didn't get into the Ritz-Carlton, which was a Bradley method class, but we did get into the less glamorous, hospital-run class (we'll call this the Marriott). A labor/delivery nurse taught the class, and I was pleasantly surprised that she strongly encouraged us all to try drug-free delivery. She'd had several children without medication herself, yet she totally realized that some women won't do it sans drugs. She taught basic information mainly centered on what the stages of childbirth are, how you might control your pain with breathing, and what your partner might do to help. Any class you enroll in will teach these basics too. Explore your options, though, and take what resonates with you. Just don't stress over it too much.

For Class Phobes

Some people are absolutely what I call class phobic. Our neighbors were that way. They went to their first birthing class and couldn't bear the thought of going back. Instead, they went online and read all they could about labor and delivery. And, yes, the birth of their daughter went perfectly. Another friend's husband really couldn't deal with the classes either, so they decided to have a two-session private class. Again, the birth of their daughter was great.

My husband is admittedly not someone who likes to take classes. He once drove our dog to obedience class, saw all the other dog owners outside the pet store sitting on lawn chairs, and drove away. So he wasn't particularly enthusiastic about going to birthing class each Thursday evening for two months. I "strongly encouraged" him, though, and he survived and actually seemed to enjoy it sometimes. We still both like the photo taken at the class where he's wearing the fake pregnancy stomach (they do that to give the dads a little taste of what it's like to be pregnant—as if that's even close to the experience!).

The main benefit I saw in going to the class was that it gave us an opportunity to get out together and focus on the fact that we were about to bring a child into the world. So if your partner or you is class phobic, maybe you can think of it this way too. It's like date night—only the type of movie you're going to see is one of women in labor. By the way, don't fear the videos. They're all designed to be reassuring.

A Minor Problem with Childbirth Classes

FEARLESS Midwife

Childbirth classes are important for providing information on the pregnancy and what may transpire during labor and delivery. The biggest problem that I see with classes, though, is the amount of responsibility couples feel burdened with as a result. Women worry that they won't breathe right. Men worry that they won't be able to control their partners during labor. Many couples decide they want to attempt labor without pain medication, and they take classes to teach them how to do this. Then they worry that if they change their minds, they won't be allowed to have medication. In other words, sometimes the very classes designed to reassure you open a Pandora's box of worries.

Relax. Classes should provide you with basic information and a few coping skills. If, when you're in labor, you don't remember what you've learned, or if your breathing or relaxation techniques aren't cutting it, your doctor, midwife, or nurse will step in. It's our job to help you through the process.

A final thought about classes in general: I firmly believe the more important classes in life are parenting classes. Labor is one day of your life. Raising your child is every day for the rest of your life, and your child's emotional well-being is forever.

Shopping for Childbirth Classes

Most first-time parents nowadays take some sort of prenatal class (or classes). Ask your health care provider for a list of classes in your area. And don't hesitate to shop around for the program that suits your needs best. If you're picky about which class you take, definitely shop early (maybe even in the middle of your second trimester), because some classes fill up fast.

FIVE POINTS TO CONSIDER

1. At what point in your pregnancy are classes scheduled? You may find early pregnancy classes that offer a chance to learn interesting information on birth choices and caregivers when you are making those decisions, but sessions on the actual birth are best left to the end of your pregnancy so that the information and techniques are fresh. If you're really gung-ho, also consider parenting classes in the middle of the pregnancy. They'll address issues about making lifestyle changes and getting ready for the baby, giving you something to do other than obsess over your pregnancy!
2. How large are the groups? You might like very large groups because you get to meet more future parents. Then again, smaller, more intimate groups are usually more effective educationally. Figure out what suits you.
3. Does a single educator or a team lead the program? It's nice to form a bond with a single educator for the whole series, but a team-taught approach will enable you to meet various people with whom you may wish to consult later (such as a maternal and child health nurse, a midwife, a lactation consultant, etc.). The best scenario may be a single educator who invites special guest speakers.
4. What philosophy is taught? Natural childbirth programs are ideal for some, but many women will prefer a hybrid class that encourages them to do what's required for a healthy birth and educates them about all the options.

5. What resources are available? Will there be a lending library, background research information, phone numbers of useful support agencies, and an after-hours number for the educator if you have questions?

Finding a Pediatrician

An important step in preparing for your baby is finding a pediatrician. Your caregiver should have a list of like-minded pediatricians he or she can refer you to. Also, many women get referrals from girlfriends and family members who already have children.

FEARLESS DOC

Like all medical specialties, pediatrics has doctors who run the gamut from rigid, by-the-book types to natural, laid-back ones. Seek out the kind you feel most closely suits your personality. Most pediatricians are delighted to meet you and your partner in consultation during the last few months of your pregnancy. This way both parties can decide if they are comfortable with one another.

I recommend that you ask some general questions. You want to make sure you click with the doctor's personality. A very important point, I think, is that the doctor not act defensive when you ask questions. Here are some questions to consider:

- "What are your office hours?" If you plan to go back to work, make sure there are office hours that will suit your family.
- "If my child is sick, are same-day appointments typically available?" Of course, you want the answer to be yes.
- "How strongly do you support breast-feeding? Do you refer to a lactation specialist if there's a problem?" This is important for breast-feeding and non-breast-feeding moms. You want to make sure your pediatrician supports what you plan to do.
- "How do you feel about antibiotic use in kids?" You want to pick up on whether the doctor is overly zealous about antibiotics. It's recommended that antibiotics be used extremely prudently.
- "Do you have weekend and night call coverage?" Ideally, "yes!"
- "Are you supportive of alternative medicine?" If that's not your thing, you don't want someone who leans toward diet and supplements. If you're open to this, you want someone who is also open-minded about it and perhaps knowledgeable about alternative care.

- "How do you feel about vaccinations?" Will the doctor be flexible if you do not want to vaccinate?
- "Is there an isolation waiting area for kids sick with an airborne contagious illness?" Ideally, there will be.

Induction, Induction What's Your Function?

FEARLESS DOC

For a multitude of reasons some patients will undergo induction of labor. Some will do this by choice and others for medical necessity. Common reasons for inductions of labor include being overdue (41+ weeks), diabetes, macrosomia, prolonged rupture of membranes, elevated blood pressure, developing preecclampsia, or simply being overly uncomfortable. For early medical induction and for nonemergent elective inductions before 39 weeks, your practitioner may suggest confirming your baby's lung maturity by performing an amniocentesis. Unlike a genetic amniocentesis in the second trimester, the only real risk to this amnio is that it may start labor. This isn't much of a risk, though, since you're getting the amnio because you want labor to start anyhow. Once the results are back, all options discussed, and you have agreed to proceed, your practitioner will perform a cervical check to determine how favorable your cervix is.

When the cervical exam is favorable you will most likely be started directly on Pitocin by intravenous drip. Sometimes, simply rupturing the membranes alone will be sufficient to start labor. When your cervix isn't favorable, you will probably be given, intravaginally, a medication called prostaglandin. This is not used in asthmatics or when you have had previous uterine surgery such as a c-section or fibroid removal (myomectomy). After one or more doses of this medication you will either be in labor or you will also be given Pitocin.

Stories abound about the evils of inductions and especially Pitocin. Like most stories they are usually sensationalized or they wouldn't be interesting. I tell my patients that good contractions cause discomfort whether spontaneous or from Pitocin.

Patients who are induced for medical necessity do have a higher c-section rate. This is not from the medicine itself but from the fact that the reason you are being induced already puts you into a category or diagnosis that carries a higher risk for c-section. Most importantly, being well informed allows you to know what to expect and this knowledge goes a long way toward alleviating the fears and misinformation that the word "induction" carries with it.

FEAR: The birth won't go the way I want it to.

FEARLESS FACT: Select your practitioners well, and it likely will.

First, a caveat: A wise midwife once told me that births can't be planned the same way that, say, a wedding is planned. Many women want fairy tale weddings, and they get them because they plan meticulously for a year and pay whatever it takes to have what they want. But no matter how well you plan and whom you pay to do what, you simply can't ensure the birth of a human being will go 100 percent according to plan. Well, it will go according to *a* plan; it just may not be *your* plan.

That said, there are certainly great ways to help ensure that all goes well: Have a detailed birth plan and select a doctor and/or midwife with whom you feel extremely comfortable. With these two things in place, you can't ensure that your best friend won't get stuck in traffic and miss the birth by minutes or that you won't need Pitocin to help move your labor along, but the odds are excellent that you'll be happy with the results.

What's Pitocin?

Pitocin is the synthetic version of the maternal hormone oxytocin, which occurs naturally in your body throughout pregnancy. You become much more sensitive to it, though, as you approach delivery. The drug, administered through an i.v., is often used to jump-start a stalled labor and is also sometimes used with other medications to induce labor. There are no real side effects for your baby or you, but because it makes contractions more productive, it may make the experience more intense. If you need pain relief, don't hesitate to ask.

The Cord Strangle Question

FEARLESS DOC

Every week I can count on hearing this question at least once: "Will my baby strangle itself on the umbilical cord because it moves so much?" Or this one: "Is my baby moving so much because he or she is choking on the umbilical cord?" The answer to both of these questions is *no.* If your baby is moving, your baby is doing fine!

What's a Birth Plan?

A birth plan is a guide for your health care team that details what your partner and you would like to have happen during your labor and delivery. Some doctors and midwives will present you with a form toward the end of your pregnancy and discuss the various options (if you don't get one, use the questions that follow).

Some of the questions on the form are silly. Would you like to wear your own nightgown or the hospital gown? When you're not in labor, you might actually think you'd care about this. The question is silly, though, because when you're in labor, believe me, you won't give two shakes what you're wearing or how you look.

Other questions you will care about, though. Would you like to have pain medication? Are you going to try to breast-feed? Even if you tell your doctor or midwife that you'd like to do it one way, however, don't think you can't change your mind. The birth plan is simply a wish list of how you'd ideally like the birth to proceed. And even though you've made your birth plan, it's always wise to keep an open mind and realize that the main goal is to end the day with a healthy baby and healthy mom.

What I discovered is that much of my plan was already fairly well decided based on who I had chosen for a health care practitioner and which birthing scenario I had selected. (For me, it was a midwife and doctor in a hospital, but many of you will choose a birth center or home birth.) I just looked at the birth plan as material for discussion at one of my doctor's visits. I didn't bother discussing nightgowns, because I thought that wasn't important. And I didn't bother discussing fetal monitoring and many other areas, because I trusted my doctor and midwife enough to feel sure they would let me know when certain procedures were necessary. I did discuss whether I wanted pain medication and whether I was planning to breast-feed.

I once attended a La Leche League meeting and heard the group instructor say that hospital personnel often ignore birth plans. She recommended baking a batch of cookies while in labor and bringing them to the hospital with your birth plan and a note attached asking that the nurses please follow your wishes. I think this is going overboard. (Pretty please, don't bake cookies while you're in labor unless, of course, you want to eat them!)

By and large, hospital personnel are not out to get you or make your birth experience miserable. And you're not going to be knocked out and unable to say anything. They'll ask you or your partner questions (such as "Do you want to try to breast-feed or do you want me to get a bottle of formula?"), and then you'll answer. My advice is to use these points and questions as a springboard for discussion with your doctor or midwife.

A Sample Birth Plan

Here is an example of a typical birth plan questionnaire. You'll likely be told to go through a similar questionnaire and mark "yes" for the options you want and "no" for those you don't.

LABOR

_____ Wear own nightgown
_____ Electronic fetal monitoring test trace on admission
_____ Consent to be a teaching patient (students/staff present at any time)
_____ Return home if not in established labor
_____ Food/fluids on request throughout labor
_____ Intravenous drip in labor
_____ External fetal monitoring throughout labor
_____ Internal fetal monitoring if needed
_____ Monitoring fetal heart rate by hand (fetal stethoscope)
_____ Freedom to choose positions and activity in labor (walking, sitting, squatting, etc.)
_____ Vaginal exam for specific medical indication only
_____ Full information on risks and benefits of each suggested medical procedure
_____ Artificial rupture of the membranes
_____ Artificial hormone (oxytocin) to boost contractions or induce labor
_____ Access to water pool, shower, or bath for pain relief

_____ Medication for pain in labor

Medication preferred: ______________________________

_____ Partner/chosen person(s) present at all times

_____ Siblings present for labor

BIRTH

_____ Presence of partner/chosen person(s) during actual birth

_____ Siblings present for birth

_____ Partner/chosen person(s) present for cesarean birth

_____ Birth in same room as labor

_____ Position for second stage chosen by mother

_____ Pushing begun on mother's urge only

_____ No draping of mother with sheets for the birth

_____ Pain medication for delivery

Medication preferred: ______________________________

_____ No specific time limit on second stage if progress is being made

_____ Episiotomy

_____ Freedom to touch baby during birth

_____ Father/mother assisting with actual birth by hand

_____ Midwife to assist baby's birth

_____ Baby allowed to take first breaths unassisted (no immediate suctioning, etc.)

_____ Late cord clamping (after pulsating stops)

_____ Skin-to-skin contact for mother and father with baby immediately after birth

_____ Artificial hormone injection (oxytocin) after the birth to expel the placenta

_____ Baby on breast to stimulate expulsion of placenta

_____ Vernix left on

_____ Baby weighed, measured in parents' presence after initial bonding period

POSTNATAL

_____ Baby remains with mother at all times (nights included)

_____ Person of choice in mother's room at any time of day

_____ Breast-feeding on demand from birth

_____ Help with breast-feeding on request

_____ Formula feeding
_____ Vitamin K for baby: oral/injection/withheld unless requested
_____ Eye ointment for baby
_____ Vaccines, in particular hepatitis B
_____ Circumcision
_____ Early discharge from hospital as soon as mother wishes
_____ Additional ideas: ________________________________

The Importance of Like Minds

FEARLESS Midwife

Trust and feeling secure will play important roles in your labor and delivery. Fear can inhibit many of our bodily functions and can impact your birth process. Whatever you can do to make yourself feel more secure, that's what you should do. For example, some people feel more at ease in a hospital, while others feel more secure with a home birth. If you do decide on a hospital, visit the birthing rooms, meet some nurses, and familiarize yourself with the setting beforehand. On the big day, bring photos from home, your own pillows, some favorite music, and anything else that will make you feel better.

I've had grown women show up with their blankies from childhood. Whatever works. Having trust in your health care practitioner will go a long way to ease fear. I realize most women are somewhat restricted by insurance coverage, but hopefully you've been able to find a team you believe is competent and reassuring. If you haven't, perhaps there's still time to do this. It's important to trust that you're getting good advice and care.

Love Comes in Different Forms

FEARLESS DOC

Preparing for delivery wouldn't be complete without a word about preparing your husband or partner. In my experience, men come in many forms. There are the ones who come to every doctor appointment and the ones I meet for the first time in the labor room. Some partners cringe at the sight of blood, and others want to help with hands on at the delivery. Some wipe the brow and offer the mother nourishment, while others watch the game or read the paper. I think it's wise to remember that love comes in many forms, and there's no one way the dad should act.

What Should I Do, Honey?

As taxing as delivery is for most women, it's also taxing for men. For months leading up to the birth of our son, my husband kept asking me what I might want him to do during labor. Of course, we'd gone to birthing classes and learned about the various options (reminding me to breathe was the big one), but he still seemed unsure of how he was truly going to help.

The problem was, I was also unsure. I couldn't give him a great answer because I simply didn't know what I'd want him to do. In the end, I told him to keep cool and not try to make me laugh, because that would likely backfire. I realize now that was a pretty strange job description, but he did it, and on our way out of the hospital the head nurse stopped to tell me that she thought he was going to make an excellent father because he was so calm.

As long as guys are aware and are as attentive as possible, I don't think they can lose. They may not win—as in, they may not always say exactly what you want to hear, or they may not be able to be the knight in shining armor that makes all the pain and difficulty go away—but they certainly can't fail as badly as they may fear.

Relax, Men (but Not Too Much)

FEARLESS Midwife

My favorite joke about labor goes like this:

The midwife gets a frantic call from a husband who screams, "My wife's contractions are three minutes apart, what do I do?" The midwife replies calmly, "Is this her first child?" "No!" he screams again, "this is her husband!"

So, yes, sometimes men become a little rattled during labor. It's understandable and forgivable. Guys, please note, however, that you are not expected to control your partner. The medical professionals are there to help. The most important thing for you to do is just be nice and do whatever your partner tells you to do. But don't turn on the TV, eat McDonalds, or talk on your cell phone without her permission. I hear those things are a little harder to forgive.

Doulas to the Rescue!

There is a sure-fire way to ensure the heat is off your hubby during the birth: hire a doula. Think of a doula as a step far above your medical training and experience (which is probably close to zilch) but definitely less than the highly trained and experienced midwives and, of course, OB/GYNs.

My very smart friends Jane and Jenna both hired doulas and highly recommend that everybody who can afford one do so. Jane's and Jenna's doulas ensured that the mothers were as comfortable as possible and also offered reassurance, support, and information throughout the labor and delivery process. Prices differ based on where you live, but doulas may be around $1,000. You can also hire a doula to help out at home with the newborn.

DOULA DEFINED

The word "doula" comes from the Greek word for the most important female servant in an ancient Greek household, the woman who probably helped the lady of the house through her childbearing. The word has come to refer to a woman experienced in childbirth who provides continuous physical, emotional, and informational support to the mother before, during, and just after childbirth.

FEAR: I won't know when I go into labor.

FEARLESS FACT: Even if you don't know at first, it won't take long before you do.

When I first woke my husband and said I thought I was in labor, it took a long time before he actually agreed with me. He got a piece of paper and a clock with a second hand and tried to keep track of my contractions. But when they took too long or were far-spaced he said, "Oh, it's probably false labor." It seemed as if he were trying to talk me out of believing it, even though it was after my due date.

Of course, I had my own part in the denial process. I'd say, "Well, I think this is a contraction. No, wait. It stopped. No, no, it didn't." In retrospect, this sounds nuts. Of course I was in labor! We both knew it, but we spent an hour or so grappling with the reality. It's perfectly okay if you want to do the same.

When your labor first starts, you may pretend you're not in labor. But the fact is that when it's crucial that you know, there will be no mistaking it. It's not going to feel like a mosquito bite in your side. It usually starts out sort of crampy, but as it progresses, Mother Nature ensures that you feel something big so that, just in case you're confused, you'll know the baby isn't; he's on his way.

First babies generally take anywhere from six to eighteen hours to make it here (even twenty-four isn't unreasonable). Don't worry. You'll have enough time to not believe you're in labor and then believe it.

Don't Panic, Okay?

FEARLESS Midwife

Your water breaks in the middle of the night without warning, and suddenly you're a quivering mess of nerves, shock, and outright panic. Now what? Your partner runs for the childbirth class notebook and looks up what to do next, when suddenly a contraction hits. He takes one look at your face, runs for the phone, and dials ... his mother. You laugh, but believe me, it has happened. The most important thing in labor is to remain calm. Babies don't just fall out. It takes many hours and a lot of hard work to get a baby out.

Three Stages of a "Typical" Vaginal Delivery

FEARLESS DOC

Everyone is different, but here's a rough idea of what to expect:

1. Being in labor: Usually, this is a bit of a marathon and lasts many hours, during which your contractions get progressively stronger, your water breaks (or is broken), and your cervix goes from zero to ten centimeters on the dilation scale. The last phase is the notorious one. It's called transition. Transition is the painful part with contractions lasting sixty to ninety seconds and occurring about every two to three minutes. Good news: Transition is usually the shortest stage of your labor. Afterwards, you're ready to push!
2. Delivering the baby: You'll have a distinctive urge to push, caused by the pressure of your baby's head. First-time moms will usually have to push about one to three hours. The uterine contractions are sixty to ninety seconds long, with intervals of two to four minutes. Good news: You get a big reward for your efforts.
3. Delivering the placenta: After you have the baby, who cares about the placenta? Everybody but you. Your doctor or midwife will look for signs that your placenta is separating from the uterine wall and moving down into the vagina. He or she will pull gently on the cord and press above your pelvis to help expel it and then will examine the placenta to make sure all of it has come out. Good news: You probably won't feel or care much about any of this. Usually, you will be given the hormone drug oxytocin. This speeds your uterine contractions after the birth and helps in delivering the placenta and ensuring against unnecessary blood loss. By the way, this (along with vacuums, forceps, and c-sections) is a large part of why childbirth is so safe these days.

See also A Typical Cesarean Delivery, *page 207, and* Forceps and Vacuums, *page 200.*

FEAR: I won't be able to handle the pain.

FEARLESS FACT: If you can't, there's help.

My birthing class had a reunion a few months after the completion of our class. All of us, of course, shared our birthing stories. This is what I learned: You can't guess ahead of time who will ultimately deliver with or without pain medication.

Most of us went into it trying for a drug-free childbirth. Some of us did it. But it wasn't the toughest or even the seemingly most determined moms who didn't get pain medication. In fact, the most soft-spoken and frail-looking woman of the group fared the best. The pain made so little impact on her that she said she told her husband she was ready to have another baby right afterward! Others of us, well…let's just say we'd learned to appreciate the word epidural, and we were not ready to have another baby, at least for a while.

If you have a goal to give birth without drugs, don't think you can't do it. But do know that there is medication to help, and there's no shame in partaking of it.

FROM THE FEARLESS DOC:

More About Pain

What's a Natural Delivery?

Often, people use the term "natural delivery" in a confusing and even insulting way. For instance, they may say that someone who has an unmedicated water birth had a "natural" birth, but someone who gives birth in the hospital with pain medication didn't. Nothing could be further from the truth. An underwater birth any way you look at it isn't natural (we're not reptiles). That doesn't mean I don't support water births. It's just that I think we should reevaluate how we use the term "natural." All vaginal deliveries, with or without pain medication, are natural.

What's an Epidural?

Used in both vaginal and cesarean deliveries, this is the most popular anesthetic for labor. An epidural is a local pain block, which means you have decreased sensation from your waist down, but you're still awake and alert. The anesthesia used in an epidural can't enter your baby's blood stream.

Furthermore, even though it's administered through a tiny tube in your back (sounds grosser than it feels), women who have epidurals do not have a greater number of back problems later. Some women, regardless of whether they've had epidurals or not, experience postpartum back pain, but that's not due to drugs. It's due to weakened abdominal muscles from the pregnancy.

Something to Know about Pain Medication

Having a totally nonmedicated childbirth experience is the goal for many women. Sometimes, despite these desires, their bodies don't end up coping well with the pain. The pain they feel, even though they are doing their best to grin and bear it, causes increased voluntary muscle resistance. This means that in some women, every time they have a contraction, they fight it rather than go with it. This makes it harder for the baby's head to come down. Sometimes the best idea is to give in and have pain medication so that the birth can progress.

THE MOST PAINFUL (AS IN ANNOYING) QUESTION IN THE LABOR UNIVERSE

How do you handle pain? In the months and weeks leading up to delivery, more than a few people might ask you this. They're searching for a way that will lead them—and you—to decide something about how your labor and delivery might go.

The question never made sense to me. What pain? A headache feels different to me than a paper cut. And both of those feel different than having a tooth drilled while Novocaine is wearing off, which likely feels different from labor. My advice is to forget even trying to answer this question. Pain comes in so many different forms and different degrees that it's impossible to answer. Also, you'd be shocked at how many women claim that they are total wimps and don't handle pain at all, but then they are able to have a baby without medication. And, of course, it also happens the other way around. Many women say they "handle pain well" and won't need anything to take the edge off, and then they decide they do.

FROM THE FEARLESS MIDWIFE

Pain: A Necessary Evil

There is good news about pain in labor: it has a purpose. Often the pain means that your labor is progressing, and that, of course, is what we want. I commend women who can get through it without pain medication, and I commend women who get through labor with it. In other words, whatever works.

Some women breeze through labor and birth quite easily; others don't. Our bodies are all different, and many factors figure in. Whether you have an easier time or not sometimes has to do with the size of the mother in relation to the baby, but it also has to do with the baby's position, the effectiveness of the uterine contractions, the shape of the pelvis, and a myriad of other factors. The important thing to remember is that any woman who gives birth, whether vaginally or abdominally, with pain medication or without, has performed a profoundly glorious miracle.

As a midwife I strongly believe that our bodies were meant to give birth, but I'm also glad that gone are the days when women in labor were tied down with nothing but a knife under the bed to symbolically "cut the pain."

Cell Banks and Blood Banks

SHOULD YOU BANK STEM CELLS?

Sometime during your pregnancy, you will receive information from your practitioner regarding the collection of umbilical cord blood for stem cell banking. I'm often asked about the worthiness and the cost of this process. Here is what I tell my patients.

Stem cell research is in its infancy right now. There are reported cases of cord blood stem cells being used successfully in transplants mainly for blood cell cancers (such as leukemia, aplastic anemia, etc.). It's likely that in the future, as our knowledge and technology expand, there will be many more uses for this easily collected specimen.

Cord blood stem cell collection is performed at delivery after the cord is cut by draining the stem cell–rich fetal blood from the placenta. The blood is then sent to a facility that separates out the stem cells and freezes them for long-term preservation. The initial cost for this procedure varies among companies and runs between $800 and $1,800. There is also a yearly storage fee of around $100.

The only downside to collecting cord blood is the question of its cost versus its value. The risk of your child or a close relative developing a condition requiring a stem cell transplant is admittedly rare. It boils down to whether you can afford it. If you can, it makes sense to sign up for the procedure during your pregnancy so that you are prepared to have your practitioner collect the blood at birth.

SHOULD YOU BANK YOUR BLOOD?

Autologous blood donation is the practice of storing your own blood early in your pregnancy in anticipation of the very rare instance when you may need a transfusion because of heavy bleeding after delivery. There was a trend to recommend this in the late 1980s and early 1990s due to the fear of blood products being contaminated with the AIDS virus. I no longer recommend this because the risk of hemorrhage requiring a transfusion in pregnancy is only about one in four hundred, and with new tests and blood banking protocols, there is no longer a statistically significant risk of transmitting HIV or hepatitis. Should this subject come up with your practitioner, you can feel very comfortable saying no thank you.

FEAR: My baby or I will die during delivery.

FEARLESS FACT: Giving birth is extremely safe, especially since there are instruments, procedures, and medications to ensure that safety.

It used to be common that women died in childbirth. Now, when you give birth in the United States with proper medical attention, the chances of anything terrible happening are so rare that it's barely worth writing two sentences about. But I will:

1. You won't die, and neither will your baby.
2. Your doctor and/or midwife want the same happy outcome you want, and they'll ensure there is one.

Okay, here's a third: Check out the sections that follow on External Fetal Monitors, Internal Monitors, Forceps and Vacuums, and Cesarean Births.

From the Fearless Doc: Childbirth Technology

External Fetal Monitors

Almost all women who have babies in hospitals and birthing centers will be put on a fetal monitor at some point. This is a device that records the baby's heart rate and pattern, as well as the frequency of your uterine contractions. Most of the time this will be done externally and will consist of two belts around your tummy that are connected to the monitor by long wires. They are easily disconnected to allow you to walk or go to the bathroom.

Your practitioner looks at the tracing to determine the baby's health in the uterus and to evaluate your contractions. Some hospitals and doctors prefer continuous monitoring, while others are content with intermittent monitoring. Your practitioner uses this information to ensure the progress of your labor as well as the baby's tolerance to it.

I've heard patients voice concerns over fetal monitoring because they read somewhere that it can lead to increased c-section rates. Many patients who have explored "alternative" birthing have been told to avoid fetal monitors and particularly to avoid continuous monitoring. This, I believe, is poor advice. It's true that studies have shown intermittent listening to the fetal heart in labor can be as accurate as continuous monitoring. For low-risk laboring patients this is certainly a viable alternative. For many, however, it's not the wisest road to take. Precise interpretation of an abnormal heart rate pattern, determined through continuous monitoring, has prevented many a heartache.

My advice is that if you trust your practitioner, you should trust his or her judgment about fetal monitoring. If you have concerns, though, discuss fetal monitoring with your doctor or midwife when you discuss your birth plan.

Internal Monitoring

On rare occasions your practitioner may also use an internal fetal monitor. This is a wire with an electrode that attaches to the baby's scalp. Another device, an intrauterine pressure catheter (IUPC), is a long plastic tube that is placed inside the uterus alongside the baby. Although the visual image of the electrode may be scary to you, it will not cause any harm to your baby, except perhaps a scratch mark or two. This device is usually placed when external monitors are not readable or not reassuring. Some common situations include obesity, meconium passage, or patterns of concern to your practitioner where more precise information is needed.

The IUPC gives more defined information concerning the strength of your contractions. It's commonly used when your labor progress is stalled and when patients are undergoing a trial of labor after a previous c-section. It can also be used for something called an amnioinfusion. This can be done when there's evidence that the umbilical cord is being compressed. By placing fluid back into the uterine cavity, you can sometimes cushion the cord and allow more time for labor to progress. Amnioinfusion is also done to dilute thick meconium passage.

Occasionally, I'll have patients tell me that they've read somewhere or have been advised by someone (not a true medical professional, I'm sure) to avoid an internal monitor because there is an increased chance of infection and of eventual c-sections. I haven't found an increased rate of infection in my patients. There is an increased rate of c-sections. It isn't from the internal monitors themselves, however, but from the underlying condition that dictates the necessity of their placement.

What's Meconium?

Meconium is a greenish-brown substance that comes from your baby's digestive system. Usually, it's passed after birth as your baby's first stool. Sometimes, especially with overdue babies or those under stress in the womb during labor, it's passed prior to delivery into your amniotic fluid.

If meconium is passed, the only thing you really know is that your baby is able to poop. It doesn't mean there's a problem. When your baby is delivered with meconium, though, more attention will be paid to suctioning the baby's mouth and nose so he or she doesn't inhale it.

Forceps and Vacuums

Forceps and vacuums—there are few other words in all of obstetrics that instill more fear and misconception. These devices have gotten a bad rap. It's unjustified, but understandable. These tools have become victims of the "plane crash syndrome." Every day thousands of planes land without incident. Once in a while, though, one crashes, and that's what we all hear about. Yet we never think of the 99.999 percent of planes that land without incident.

The same sensationalism occurs with forceps and vacuums. Rare is the report of the beautifully performed vacuum delivery that spares a mom a c-section or the expert forceps delivery of a healthy baby in trouble. The truth is that in skilled hands, these can be helpful tools for your baby and you. They are designed to coddle and protect the baby's head. It's important, though, to have a conversation with your practitioner about this possibility ahead of time. Ask how comfortable your practitioner is with these devices and how often he or she uses them. Again, it will come down to trust if the indication to use them arises.

WHAT ARE VACUUMS?

Vacuums are soft plastic cups that hold the baby's head so that when you push during a contraction, the head stays down. Your doctor can't pull too hard, since that will cause the vacuum to come off. Vacuums are helpful when the baby's head stays sideways (transverse), when you're exhausted and can't push effectively anymore, or when the baby's heart rate is depressed as the head begins to crown. There isn't any legitimate downside to using them, and the possible complications are rare.

WHAT ARE FORCEPS?

Forceps are instruments that, in proper hands, can be placed on the baby's head when the heart rate goes down for an extended period or when the head is in an abnormal position. Forceps can allow your doctor to deliver your baby in a matter of seconds if needed, which may be crucial in preventing lack of oxygen to your baby.

Forceps can be a wonderful tool in an emergency, especially in a small hospital that lacks full-time anesthesia and operating room crews for cesarean births. Though rare, forceps do have more potential to cause damage, especially to the uterus in the form of lacerations. The lesson here is that the use of forceps depends on your doctor's skill and your consent. Without both, they shouldn't enter the picture.

The Vagina Talk

Even if you don't fear contraction pain, most women have a fear of what will happen to their vaginas in the delivery process. In fact, many women obsess about this for months. I usually give them the "vagina talk" and then tell them to try to forget about it. Repress, deny, whatever—just put it out of your mind. Obsessing, visualizing, or mentally agonizing over what will happen to your vagina at the time of delivery is not a helpful thing to do.

Instead, repeat over and over, if necessary, "My body was designed to do this!" Just as your heart is designed to beat, your vagina is designed to stretch. And that is exactly what it will do.

I often compare vaginas to those Chinese shar-pei dogs. If you stretched out their skin, those dogs would be much larger than they appear. Vaginas are also made of a very wrinkly type of skin and were built to accommodate the delivery of a baby. Amazingly enough, your vagina doesn't hurt inside when it stretches; it's only at the opening where you have the pain receptors. This sensation is often referred to as "the ring of fire." Please try to remember one very important thing: This part of your labor will last only a couple of minutes, compared to hours and hours of contractions. You can do this for a few minutes. Really.

Episiotomies

Occasionally a woman will ask me to cut an episiotomy instead of risking a tear in her vagina during the delivery. An episiotomy is a procedure where the vaginal opening is cut, usually with scissors, to make it bigger to accommodate the delivery. For some women, the idea of having a cut seems more pleasant than having their skin torn.

Episiotomies are not as common or as popular as they once were, but I always say that in obstetrics there is a time and place for everything. There is a time and place for episiotomies, but they should only be done in certain cases. Normally, a tear is better. Imagine for a minute how you cut fabric. Often you make a small cut and then pull to make a long rip. This is often what happens when an episiotomy is cut; it puts you more at risk for tearing into your rectum. When your body is allowed to stretch naturally, though, the tear, if any, is usually less severe and more superficial. In my practice I have found that almost

80 percent of women don't tear at all or have only a superficial tear of the skin. Rarely has a woman ever torn into her rectum, unless an episiotomy was cut first.

Nature also has a strange way of providing a sort of anesthetic with delivery. Often, when I ask a woman after delivery to let me check to see if she has any tears, she'll say she doesn't, even though we find she does. You might imagine that any tear would continue to cause agonizing pain. That is usually not the case. Although your skin can be tender to the touch, once the baby is delivered, women don't report much pain from a tear. Local anesthetic is used to repair any tears, and ice is applied to the area. Most women have some vaginal pain after delivery, whether they had stitches or not, simply by virtue of having had a baby pass through their vaginal opening. Once again, there is medication to help, and this too will pass.

Hypnosis for Pain

FEARLESS DOC

Hypnobirthing is another option for better relaxation during labor. You will learn techniques to induce a state of relaxed concentration similar to the daydreaming that occurs when you are engrossed in a book or staring at a fire. You're aware of your surroundings and can carry on a conversation while you control your body's sensation of pain. Classes are taught by certified hypnobirthing instructors who can be found via the Internet. I've had experience with patients who have done wonderfully with this technique and some for whom it was unsuccessful but did well after epidural placement.

Cesarean Sections

FEAR: I'll need a c-section.

FEARLESS FACT: The odds are against it, but even if you have one, it won't be unnecessary, and you'll recover well.

Most women don't know much about c-sections, but they do know they don't want one. What you imagine happening—an incision being made somewhere in your mid-section and the baby being extracted—is admittedly not too enticing. My niece Jennifer heard the words "possible c-section" while she was in the delivery room, and she said this is what got her to finally give the productive pushes that allowed her to deliver her daughter. So the threat of a c-section actually motivated her.

I was not really afraid of having a c-section. I'd been in the room when my friend Donna had one and got to see the procedure firsthand. It made an impact on me (as watching any birth will), but it wasn't horrifying. The doctors and Donna were all in good spirits. Her son was born beautifully, and I didn't see the experience as something abnormal or traumatic. Yet I didn't count on having one myself.

I paid lip service to the possibility, of course. I remember telling my husband a week or so before we had our son that some women end up getting c-sections. He dismissed the idea. Like me, he didn't think there was much of a possibility that I'd need one. The baby wasn't getting too large, the pregnancy had gone well, and we'd both known plenty of women of all shapes and sizes who gave birth the regular old way without incident. What happened?

Well into my labor—around the time I thought our son would soon be coming out one way—we were told that he'd actually need to come out by another route. I had a c-section, and at the time I was glad I had the option, because it was medically necessary. About 25 percent of births go this way, although this number is a bit misleading because it includes repeat c-sections, and the rate of repeat c-sections is much higher than that of first-time c-sections.

Many OBs strive to avoid c-sections. To increase your odds of not having one, though, make sure your doctor understands that you want one only as a last resort and verify that he or she agrees with this philosophy. If you need one, you'll get one, of course. And while you may suffer some emotional fallout (I would describe my reaction afterward more as shock than grief, but I definitely had to grapple with the "why me?" question), before long you will move on. Some women say they feel as though they were ripped off by not having the birthing experience.

All these feelings are valid, but in the end we must try to think and act like good mothers. What would a good mother say to her daughter if she had to have a c-section? She'd tell her that the goal in all of this was to end the day with a healthy baby and a healthy mom. When the goal is achieved, there's a lot to be grateful for and not a ton to complain about.

The C-Section Discussion

FEARLESS DOC

Many women have significant concerns about not being able to deliver their baby "naturally" and fear they will end up with a cesarean section. Experience tells me this fear is a cause of much subtle stress throughout the nine months.

It is a fact that cesarean section rates in this country currently average more than 20 percent and are rising. Realize, though, that one of the main contributors to this increase is the current trend toward repeat cesarean sections instead of attempts at vaginal birth after having had a cesarean section.

If you have already had a c-section, your odds of a vaginal delivery are still very good. However, you should have a discussion with your doctor about your concerns. Let him or her know that you only want a c-section as a last resort. Try to feel your doctor out. You obviously need another caregiver if the one you have seems to want to schedule a c-section as a matter of convenience. Once you have a like-minded caregiver, you can rest assured you won't have an unnecessary c-section. In the event that you do need a c-section, though, understand that you may ask for the following, which may make the situation better:

- Ask that your baby be brought to your chest as soon as possible, even while your doctor is finishing your surgery. Also ask if you can have the baby in the recovery room with you. (Note that the hospital may not allow this, but it's worth requesting.)

- Request that your doctor use sutures instead of staples on your outer incision. Sutures are a little neater, and you won't need to have them removed a week afterward.
- After a day or so, you may want to switch from the narcotic painkillers to Motrin. You will feel less foggy this way and may be able to enjoy your baby more. But don't do this if your pain isn't manageable.

Cesarean Births

FEARLESS DOC

No matter how hard you try or how much you desire a natural birth, some of you will end up with a cesarean delivery. Some women experience this as a loss. I've had patients who have also said they felt like it was a failure of their womanhood. If words have power and I can do one good thing with my words in this book, it would be to help those few realize what a wonder they've just created. Through no fault of their own, their best-laid plans did not turn out the way they envisioned them. Nature does this, and each of us must find the good in it.

Less than 100 years ago, women and children died in childbirth at an alarming rate. Because of c-sections, this doesn't happen anymore. Unless you are scheduled to have an elective c-section, there is just no good way to plan for one. Oh, you can be well educated about them, but it's hard to plan for something you don't expect and don't want. Just know that if you find yourself having a c-section, you will recover, albeit more slowly than from most vaginal deliveries.

Complications from c-sections are rare, but your hospital stay will likely be three or four days rather than one or two. You will be a bit more sore and slower to move, and you'll be asked to refrain from driving for a couple of weeks. But, really, where are you going to go anyway? You may require some stronger pain medication, but I find that's often not the case and that something like Motrin is all that is needed postoperatively. Yes, you'll have a scar, but your vagina will be spared a bit of stretching. Breast-feeding will be the same and, after the first hour or two, so will bonding. Many hospitals are finally wising up to consumer wishes and are allowing c-section mothers and their babies to be together in a special recovery area after delivery. Ask your hospital about this, even if you don't ultimately have a c-section. If hospitals get enough women asking, they may consider making this option available.

Finally, you'll have to abstain from strenuous exercise for six weeks, but even women who have vaginal deliveries aren't exercising much sooner than this.

My experience is that women who've had c-sections recover at different rates based on motivation, age, and medical condition, but they all recover.

A TYPICAL CESAREAN DELIVERY

A c-section usually takes about an hour, but your baby is delivered within the first five to ten minutes, and the rest of the time is spent sewing you up. Upon entering the surgery room, you're given an epidural or a spinal, your pubic area is shaved, your bladder is drained with a catheter, and your abdomen is swabbed with antiseptic. You can request that all of these things be done after you're numb.

In surgery, your OB makes a short, horizontal incision along your bikini line, the abdominal muscles are pulled aside (not cut), and a similar horizontal incision is made in the lower segment of your uterus. The amniotic fluid is suctioned off, and your baby is gently lifted out. Then the cord is cut, your placenta is removed, and you're stitched or stapled up.

After a C-Section

The one thing that for me verged on being annoying was that when people heard that I'd had a c-section, they'd say, "Oh, I'm so sorry." I think other people's reactions can feed a new mom's feelings of having somehow failed by having the c-section. Some people, though, said, "Well, that's how it went. I'm just glad your baby and you are doing so well." I really appreciated those comments.

So if you have a c-section, be prepared for other people to pity you because they think that's the kindest thing to do. When I felt like it, I just said that I was glad the option existed, because I had needed it. Then I told them my baby and I were doing really well. If you don't have a c-section but you know someone who does, try not to pity her; try to celebrate her baby the way you should.

The Post-cesarean Discussion

Often, c-sections take you by surprise. In the heat of the situation, you sign the consent form and want the baby out by any means necessary! Of course, if this happens, it will mean that you really needed the c-section. But it doesn't mean the subject is closed for discussion.

You will likely see your doctor a week after your c-section to get your staples removed if you've had them (don't worry; it doesn't hurt). Some doctors close your skin with an absorbable suture, though, and these aren't removed. At this time, or at your six-week postpartum visit, feel free to ask questions. You may need more clarity about why you needed the cesarean, or you may want to ask about the odds of having a vaginal delivery should you have another child in the future.

Elective Cesarean Sections

FEARLESS DOC

The issue of women electing to have cesarean deliveries without any medical indication has gotten a lot of press lately. This may be a case of media sensationalism, because my colleagues and I rarely come across women who want c-sections. It's usually quite the opposite.

If you find that you want a c-section without really needing one, this is a tip-off that you're acting and thinking out of fear. Thoroughly discuss the pros and cons with your health care team. Vaginal deliveries are always safer and easier than c-sections *unless there is a medical indication for a c-section.* Once you know the facts, you'll most likely opt for a vaginal delivery. Still, there are those very, very few women who would still like a c-section, and I'm among the doctors who believe those patients' requests should be honored.

C-Section Fear

FEARLESS Midwife

For some women, the fear of a cesarean is the fear of surgery and hospitals. We know from statistics that for most women and babies, a vaginal delivery is safer. But the truth is, cesareans are quite safe too. If you have to have a cesarean, chances are slim that anything negative will happen to you.

For some women, though, a c-section is viewed as a failure because they couldn't give birth naturally. They may feel that they missed out on a physical experience that was very important for them. I liken these thoughts to wanting to climb Mount Everest. Many of us seem to have these strong biological urges to accomplish a physical feat—running a marathon, climbing a mountain, or giving birth. Some of us will do what we want to do, and some of us will need to be airlifted several feet from the finish line. It is a profound disappointment and often difficult to overcome emotionally. Try to remember, however, that birth, first and foremost, needs to be about your baby's (and your own) safety and life. Try to find solace in knowing that you made decisions that were in the best interest of your baby and probably yourself as well. In my book, a cesarean is just a different way to have a baby. You can start training for the marathon after your postpartum period.

After a C-Section: Your Next Baby

FEARLESS DOC

Prior to 2003, vaginal birth after a c-section (VBAC) was strongly advocated for selected patients who had their previous cesarean section because of breech presentation or fetal distress. There was a success rate of nearly 80 percent of these cases. Even patients who had a c-section after failing to dilate in labor had a VBAC success rate close to 65 percent in subsequent pregnancies. Many studies showed this to be a safe, viable alternative, and most physicians, hospitals, and patients embraced this opportunity.

The main risk of a VBAC is the possibility of a uterine scar rupture, causing abruption of the placenta and possible severe complications to the fetus, including death. This occurred in less than 1 percent of VBACs, and, with informed consent, the medical community felt that the patient should be able to have this choice. Remember, it was 99 percent safe and as high as 80 percent successful. The only recommendation was that emergency surgery be "readily" available. Readily was defined as within thirty minutes.

Then, in response to pressures from lawsuits, many of them frivolous, that often followed a bad outcome, and despite having proper informed consent, the American College of Obstetricians and Gynecologists changed the words in their practice guidelines from "readily available" to "immediately available." This meant that hospitals that allowed VBACs had to have obstetricians, anesthesiologists, and operating room personnel in house at all times. Most hospitals in this country do not have that luxury and, due to financial constraints, could not pay these professionals to sit around for hours on standby. Therefore, these hospitals and many physicians have decided it is not worth the liability or the financial burden to offer VBACs any longer. Thus another choice has been taken away from many patients.

Some larger institutions and university training programs do still offer VBACs. If you have this available in your community, you should discuss VBAC with your doctor to see if you're a good candidate. You and your partner will have to decide for yourselves whether this option, once considered the desirable standard of care, is right for you.

~ *Fast and Fearless*

Here's what you need to know about preparing for labor and delivery:

- Childbirth education classes can be fun and informative, but they're not mandatory (in fact, some people would argue that parenting classes are a better investment). If you hate classes, consider choosing a private session, and be sure to talk with your doctor or midwife about what to expect. Also, read up on the birth process online or in books.
- Guys, just be nice.
- Don't stress over your birth plan. Fill it out, but since you've selected your doctor/midwife and birthing scenario well, you simply must trust that they're not out to do anything against your wishes.
- Your vagina is meant to stretch—a lot!
- Don't ask for an episiotomy; a tear is almost always better than a cut.
- Unless you've already planned to have one, you probably won't have a cesarean section. But if you do, you will recover, probably much faster than you think.
- It's great to give birth without pain medication; it's great to give birth with pain medication. It's great to give birth vaginally; it's great to give birth by c-section. *It's great to give birth!*

9

Nine Common Problems—And Why You Shouldn't Fear Them

From the Fearless Doc:

Nine Common Problems

Early in your pregnancy, you'll start to hear terms such as preeclampsia or gestational diabetes. These can cause alarm or fear. Remember, any problem in pregnancy is by far the exception rather than the rule. Most pregnancies proceed without problems. But it's also reassuring to know that even if you do encounter a problem, most can be handled by a competent health care team, and the result is usually a healthy baby and mom.

Here are the nine most common pregnancy-related problems:

1. DIABETES

Gestational diabetes is a condition that develops in a small percentage of otherwise healthy pregnant women. It has to do with the pregnancy hormone human placental lactogen, which in some women instructs the body to resist insulin and causes their blood sugar to rise abnormally high after they eat. The developing baby senses these high levels of sugar and puts out his own insulin from his pancreas, which is working just fine. Insulin in the fetus acts as a growth hormone, causing the baby to grow very large, which can lead to complications at birth.

Gestational diabetes is diagnosed by glucose tolerance testing (see chapter 3) and may be suspected if you consistently test positive for sugar in your urine at your doctor visits. The condition is most commonly treated with nutritional counseling and a special diet. In rare cases, insulin injections may be required.

This type of diabetes shouldn't be confused with other forms of diabetes, because this one disappears after you deliver. While pregnant, though, you may be asked to perform finger-stick glucose testing and keep a diary of your results to share with your doctor at visits. Often, a specialist such as a perinatologist or endocrinologist will be involved in your care. Biophysical profiles to assess fetal well-being and possibly labor induction could also become part of your care plan. The outcomes in cases of diagnosed and properly managed gestational diabetes are excellent and shouldn't give you cause for alarm.

See also chapter 3 for more on diabetes, perinatologists, and biophysical profiles.

2. GROWTH RESTRICTION

In the last half of your pregnancy, your practitioner will measure your tummy at each prenatal visit. Here's the reason: there's a rough correlation between the measurement in centimeters above your pubic bone during the twentieth through the thirty-sixth week of pregnancy and the baby's growth. When the measurement seems to fall behind (or if your doctor suspects that other medical problems may hamper the growth of your baby), an ultrasound will be performed. The ultrasound is looking at measurements of the baby's head, abdomen, and leg as well as blood flow patterns that indicate growth that lags behind what's expected. When the baby falls below the tenth percentile, the condition is called "small for gestational age" (SGA). If it's below the second percentile, it's considered "intrauterine growth restricted" (IUGR).

This doesn't necessarily imply there's anything wrong with your baby, but it does mean that for the remainder of the pregnancy, your baby's growth and environment will be monitored closely. The baby may be getting poor nourishment across the placenta. In some circumstances, like decreasing amniotic fluid volume, the baby will be better off in the nursery rather than remaining in your uterus, and your doctor will recommend delivery either by inducing labor or having a cesarean section. Again, when this condition is monitored, the outcome is excellent.

3. MACROSOMIA

This word literally means "big body" in Latin. If your abdominal measurement is extremely big in the third trimester, you may be diagnosed as having a macrosomic baby. Usually, the condition will also be evaluated by ultrasound, although some studies have shown that this method is no more accurate than an estimate made by the hands of a good clinician. Uncontrolled gestational diabetes often leads to large babies (macrosomia), but sometimes it just happens when absolutely nothing is wrong.

The biggest problem with a macrosomic baby is the increased likelihood of a disproportion between the baby and your pelvis, leading to higher cesarean rates. There is also the small but real possibility of an injury to the baby at birth. If your practitioner suspects your baby is big, he or she may recommend an early induction to increase your chance of having a vaginal delivery. When the suspected weight is greater than 4,500 grams (about nine pounds and fourteen ounces), it's not uncommon for a cesarean section to be recommended. Ultimately, the choice will be yours, after you consider all the information available.

4. MULTIPLE GESTATION (TWINS, TRIPLETS, ETC.)

The incidence of spontaneous twinning is about one in every eighty pregnancies. Spontaneous triplets are exceptionally rare. Because of the increased use and success of reproductive technologies like in-vitro fertilization (IVF), however, multiple gestations have become much more common in the last decade. If you fall into this category, you will be considered a high-risk pregnancy because there are complications that can occur with multiples. Remember, though, that most of the time the following possibilities do not occur and that a twin birth can be had without problems.

The most likely complication is premature labor and delivery. Your doctor will generally recommend that you decrease your activity and avoid intercourse and orgasm in the last half of the pregnancy. You also should have more frequent health care visits and ultrasounds to check for early cervical changes and discordant growth between the babies (where one baby seems to be falling behind the other as the weeks pass).

Some doctors deliver all twin pregnancies by cesarean section, while others feel comfortable allowing you to deliver vaginally if the first twin is headfirst and the labor goes smoothly. Both are reasonable approaches and lead to the usual outcome of one big, happy family.

5. INCOMPETENT CERVIX

This is a rare problem in pregnancy where the cervix thins and dilates without contractions. It usually happens without warning and often results in the loss of the pregnancy in the second trimester. If you have a history of such a loss, or if you have had a cone biopsy for pre-cancerous changes of your cervix in the past, your practitioner may evaluate your cervical length by ultrasound throughout your pregnancy.

There are a few symptoms that may imply your cervix is prematurely opening. These include an increase in vaginal wetness that is different from your normal discharge and any pink discoloration to the discharge. If you have a history of having an incompetent cervix, or if signs appear on an ultrasound, a purse string suture—called a cerclage—will be placed by your obstetrician. You will be asked to stay in bed most of the time and avoid straining and intercourse. This will often prolong the pregnancy to a point where the baby will do quite well. The cerclage is then removed, and you can have an absolutely normal delivery.

6. PREECLAMPSIA

This condition is seen in fewer than 10 percent of pregnant patients and manifests itself as a rise in blood pressure, excessive swelling over your whole body, and the spilling of protein in the urine. For this reason, your blood pressure is checked and your urine is evaluated for protein on all of your visits to your doctor or midwife.

Not all women who develop this problem will have the classic symptoms, however. Other complaints include a headache that doesn't seem to go away with Tylenol, a lowering of your platelet count, and abnormal liver function as shown in blood tests. No one yet has discovered the reason preeclampsia happens, but the treatment is well known and usually dictated by how close you are to your due date. The treatment is to avoid salty foods and get more bed rest, being sure to lie on your side. This takes your uterus off the large vessels that run behind it and lowers your blood pressure. It allows better blood flow through your kidneys and helps to get rid of some of the fluid retention.

The real cure for preeclampsia is delivery. That's why, when the pregnancy is near term (and sometimes even if your baby is premature), your health care practitioner may recommend the induction of labor or a delivery by cesarean section. After you give birth, your symptoms usually resolve quite rapidly. Also reassuring is the fact that this usually doesn't recur in subsequent pregnancies.

7. PREMATURE LABOR

Simply put, this is defined as labor ensuing before thirty-seven weeks. Labor is defined by medical personnel as progressive effacement (thinning) and dilation of your cervix in response to regular uterine contractions.

It is not normal to have *repetitive* contractions or cramps early in your pregnancy. The most common causes of such uterine irritability are dehydration, a full bladder, and too much running around. If you feel yourself having bothersome, regular contractions, you should go to the bathroom, drink a glass or two of water or juice, and lie down for about an hour. This alone will almost always alleviate your symptoms. If it doesn't, however, call your practitioner immediately, even if it's two o'clock in the morning.

Premature labor is easier to arrest the sooner you catch it. You'll most likely be asked to go to the hospital or the office to allow monitoring of your uterus with external belts. Your cervix will be checked to see if it's changing, and your practitioner may swab a sample from the back of your vagina to send for a fetal fibronectin test and a culture for bacteria. Fetal fibronectin is a chemical that comes from the fetal membranes, and a negative test has a strong correlation with not delivering in the next two weeks. The results can be back from the lab in just a few hours at most hospitals. A positive test, however, doesn't necessarily mean you're going to have your baby soon and is therefore less useful.

If premature labor is diagnosed and your practitioner believes the baby is better off remaining in the womb, you will probably be given medication in an attempt to stop your labor. Antibiotics are given initially, and you may be asked to take a special steroid injection to help your baby's lungs more quickly get ready to breathe air should the attempts to stop your labor fail. Sometimes, there's a problem that defies medical attempts to keep the baby inside, and at other times conditions in the uterus may be so hostile that the baby will do better in the newborn care unit.

Beyond thirty-four weeks, most newborns do quite well. Newborn specialists, called neonatologists, are remarkably adept at handling earlier preemies nowadays. Although you may be frightened and disappointed, realize that if this happens, your baby will be in the hands of people who dedicate their lives to caring. Bring this positive energy with you to the nursery.

8. PLACENTA PREVIA

This rare, random condition happens about once in every 200 births. In order for your baby to deliver vaginally, he or she has to pass through the cervix. If the placenta covers the entry into the cervix, then normal delivery can't occur without the baby tearing through the placenta. That's why this is called placenta previa.

Early in pregnancy, having the placenta cover the cervix is a common finding. It only has implications if it persists. The placenta doesn't crawl around or move, but it does tend to grow upward toward areas of better blood supply and regress from areas of lesser flow near the lower parts of the uterus.

Placenta previa can easily be diagnosed as part of your second trimester genetic ultrasound. If this happens, you may be asked to refrain from sex (actually from orgasm) and diminish your activity. You'll be rechecked in six to eight weeks to see if the placenta has "moved."

If you don't have a second trimester ultrasound, or if the complication exists but isn't found, placenta previa may present itself as a frightening episode of painless, bright red, vaginal bleeding in the late second or early third trimester. Although you may be frightened by the amount of blood, this is rarely a serious threat to your baby. However, since a second bleeding episode is likely and is often more ominous, you may be hospitalized for the remainder of your pregnancy.

Sometimes your practitioner may recommend an amniocentesis around thirty-seven weeks to see if the baby's lungs are ready. Delivery will be by cesarean section, whether as an emergency or elective procedure. You will be inconvenienced, but remember that outcomes with placenta previa are almost always excellent.

9. PLACENTAL ABRUPTION

This is a rare, unpredictable event where the placenta separates either partially or entirely from the uterine wall while the baby is still inside. It's usually painful and sometimes is associated with vaginal bleeding.

The outcome of a placental abruption depends on when in the pregnancy it occurs and where you are at the time. Nevertheless, there is no reason to fear something that's so random and that you can't control.

The one situation where there is an increased incidence of abruption is after a rapid deceleration, most commonly a car accident or a bad fall. If this should happen to you, call your practitioner. She or he may suggest fetal monitoring, particularly if you're in the second half of your pregnancy.

10

Fearless Techniques for Relieving Stress

There are countless simple exercises you can do at home to help you feel calm and centered. And the more calm and centered you feel, the less likely you'll experience fears about childbirth. You can try something as simple as shutting your eyes for a few moments and focusing on your breath. Or you can try some of the other strategies we've compiled—meditations and visualizations, writing exercises, breathing techniques, and more.

Not every strategy here will appeal to you. Meditation may not hit home, for example. That's fine. Try something, and if it doesn't work for you, try something else. (That's a good tip to keep in mind, too, for impending motherhood.)

Our Top Three Favorite Ways to Alleviate Fear, Worry, and Stress

1. GET THE FACTS

There's nothing better for alleviating fear than real facts. Often, however, news reports, well-meaning friends, and some books do more to create stress than alleviate our fears. That's why we stress *real* facts. If you have a concern, bring it up with your doctor or midwife. (This is one reason you want to find a medical team that's comforting and reassuring.)

2. TALK, TALK, TALK, AND TALK SOME MORE

Talk to your doctor, midwife, partner, and friends (but, again, only the positive ones). Many women report that just being able to voice their fears and have their loved ones listen helps them immensely. Others say that just getting out and talking about anything, not necessarily the pregnancy, works wonders. It takes their minds off of themselves. If you can't seem to talk it out with friends, though, consider seeing a therapist, even for just a few sessions.

3. MOVE

Exercise is the anti-stress elixir. Walk the dog, take a yoga class, or use the treadmill. Anything that gets you moving works. Exercise has been proven time and again to alleviate stress, fear, and worry.

Express Yourself

Whether it's through journaling (not a journal written to the baby, but one meant just for you) or painting, getting creative often works miracles to relieve anxiety and even uncover buried worries. Sometimes you can focus on what's happening to you or what you're actually worried about and then write or paint about that. Try thinking of a word like "mother" or "birth" and then writing or painting anything and everything that comes to mind. No artistic training? Don't worry. Pick up a cheap box of children's watercolors and some paper and just have fun.

THE FIVE-MINUTE DAILY GIBBERISH JOURNAL

Many women are self-conscious when they write in journals. They're inhibited by punctuation, spelling, etc. When you just write freely, however, that is often the time that you find yourself expressing your true inner thoughts and feelings.

So try this: Each morning, write as much as you can in five minutes. It's better to write by hand than at the computer, but you can do it either way. The only rule is that you don't stop—not for periods, punctuation, spelling, or typos. Not to compose your thoughts or anything else! Just ramble. Write whatever comes to mind. You don't have to do anything with these thoughts. The goal is simply to get them out.

The Worry Appointment

If you find yourself worrying obsessively, here's a technique that should help. R. Reid Wilson, Ph.D., a clinical associate professor in the department of psychiatry at the University of North Carolina School of Medicine, recommends setting aside two daily sessions of ten minutes each in which you do nothing but express concerns. *Your mission: Talk out loud or speak into a tape recorder and attempt to think of no positive alternatives to your issues.* The idea is that you're giving yourself a chance to express all of your worries, even the ones you suppress.

Rod Stryker's
Baby Meditations

I interviewed Los Angeles yoga and meditation master Rod Stryker, creator of the CD *Three Meditations to Live By* (www.pureyoga.com), for these pregnancy meditations. I used his meditations often throughout my pregnancy and found them easy to do and relaxing.

One warning: Don't give up just because you try these once and feel distracted. Distraction is part of the meditation learning curve, according to Stryker. If you're new to this, expect your mind to wander at first. Slowly, you'll learn to calm down and focus. Once you get proficient, you can even do these meditations on the bus or subway with your eyes open.

Meditation One: Soothing

This exercise was designed to promote soothing and healing energy for your baby and you. Practice it once a day or as often as you need.

1. Sit comfortably with your eyes closed and concentrate on your breathing. Your mind may be restless at first, but it will eventually settle and your breathing will slow. Do this for two to five minutes (or longer, as needed).
2. Envision your body surrounded by a sense of deep calm.
3. Picture the color rose-pink. "Just as the mind and body respond to different types of music, they also respond to light and color," says Stryker. "Pastel rose is the ideal color for soothing."
4. Each time you inhale, envision rose light moving through your skin, passing deep into your body toward your spine, and ultimately reaching your baby. When you exhale, imagine rose light moving out. Continue for five minutes.
5. Stop the breathing technique, but picture yourself saturated in rose light inside and out. Remain for a few minutes or as long as you like.

Meditation Two: Calming and Healing

Just having the intention of becoming calm and embracing a state of well-being will boost your immune system and recharge your endocrine and nervous systems, according to Stryker. Again, you can practice this meditation once a day or as often as you need.

1. Sit comfortably with your eyes closed and concentrate on your breathing. Your mind may be restless at first, but it will eventually settle and your breathing will slow. Do this for two to five minutes (or longer, as needed).
2. Once your breathing is rhythmic, turn your attention to your heartbeat. You probably won't actually be able to hear or feel your heartbeat, but the idea is to direct your attention to that general area.
3. Mentally project the word "calm" to the beat of your heart. Again, this is about intention. Have the intention of slowing and calming your heartbeat.
4. When you seem to feel your heartbeat become calmer and more relaxed, move your attention to the baby. Imagine you can hear your baby's heartbeat (you won't really hear it). Mentally repeat the words "calming" and "healing."
5. Imagine what it would feel like if someone told you to create a feeling of perfect health and well-being. If a positive word spontaneously comes up for you, use and repeat that word. If you have an image or feeling come up, use those. Now mentally surround the baby with this feeling, image, or word that signifies health and well-being.
6. Envision the baby and yourself in a state of perfect health and well-being. Do this for five to ten minutes or for as long as you need.

Many people subconsciously worry and fight it, according to Wilson, author of *Don't Panic* (Harper Collins) and founder of Anxieties.com. Suppressing your concerns leads to a general feeling of anxiety. "What most people find is that when they have an appropriate time and space for their worries, it can free up the rest of their day for productive work," says Wilson.

Alternate Nostril Breathing

I know, this sounds strange (unless you've been to a yoga class where you've practiced this), but this is said to be balancing, calming, and cooling. Basically, all you do is use your right forefinger and thumb to alternate nostrils as you breathe. Take ten breaths on each side, doing this as often as needed throughout the day (or settle for just a couple of breaths while you're waiting at a stoplight). Here's a more detailed description:

1. With your right thumb, close off your right nostril and inhale deeply and slowly through your left nostril. Try to inhale to the count of four.
2. Clamp the left nostril with your forefinger and hold your breath for a count of six or so.
3. Release your thumb and let the breath out of your right nostril (again, to the count of four).
4. Start over in reverse. Breath in through your right, hold, and breathe out through your left.

Visualize the Truth

Kathryn Alice, RScP, a counselor in Venice, California, specializes in therapies with a spiritual bent. Here's what she tells her clients when they're addressing fear and worry during a session:

1. Write down everything bad that you can imagine happening. Fill an entire page, or even more if needed. The important thing is to get it out.
2. Now write the truth. For example, if you're worried about the delivery of your baby, you may have written that your baby or you will die in childbirth. The truth, of course, is that it's highly unlikely that either of you will. As you've already learned, the chances of this happening nowadays are rarer than rare. Continue writing more truths (that you have the most

competent medical team imaginable, for example, that you have faith in a higher power that is looking out for you, etc.).

3. Visualize the truth. Take time to imagine in your mind exactly how fantastic the birth will go. Imagine details if you need to: how you'll act, how your partner will respond lovingly, how your medical team will be kind and competent, etc. Each time your fear comes up regarding this issue, visualize once again what you've imagined.

The Power of Prayer, or Something Like It

Recent research has shown that prayer can have powerful effects. In one study, patients who were prayed for recuperated faster. In another study, prayer was shown to lower blood pressure. So whether you ask others to pray for you or you pray yourself, it seems you can't lose. If you're not a religious or spiritual person, try asking friends and family to merely keep you in their thoughts and wish you well.

What Real Moms Do

We asked some of our fearless mom friends to let us know how they kept their cool during pregnancy. Here's what they said:

HADLEY: ACUPUNCTURE

A few weeks before my due date, my midwife started some acupuncture on me for relaxation. It helped. I was pretty chilled about the labor and, at one point, felt like the baby could come out if I sneezed!

CELESTE: LEAN ON YOUR PARTNER

Support from my husband helped tremendously. He'd remind me to just take one step at a time and not think catastrophically.

DOROTHY: YOGA AND EDUCATION

I took prenatal yoga classes on a nearly weekly basis throughout my pregnancy, and my husband and I also took a very informative childbirth class. As I educated myself, my confidence grew.

JENNA: TALK YOURSELF DOWN

I read a lot—and I mean, a lot—which didn't help me at all. But I am the kind of person who thrives on information. In the end, I just talked myself down a lot, the same way I do when I'm flying, which I am also terrified of. I had little mantras I'd repeat: "People do this every day." "Teenagers and drug addicts manage to give birth to (relatively) healthy babies, so why wouldn't I have a healthy baby?" If I read something that said 1 percent of babies have such-and-such, I'd remind myself that 99 percent didn't.

VICKI: PAY ATTENTION TO YOUR DREAMS

I had a lot of fear about having twins and then I had a terrible dream in which I lost one of the babies. As the angel came to take the baby from me, the other twin kissed it goodbye. I realized the babies already had a unique bond inside of me. I couldn't wish to have just one baby because it would be easier for me. I realized I was blessed with a gift, and there was a reason I was chosen. This was a major turning point for me and for my attitude. By paying attention to my dream, I learned something, and my fear over having twins started to go away. I ended up enjoying my uncomplicated pregnancy so much that I was actually disappointed to see it come to an end so soon.

JANE: DEVELOP A MAGIC MANTRA

I am typically not a fearful person. For me it is more about acknowledging the fear but not embracing it. I meditated and walked. I also reframed situations in my mind. (Instead of focusing on the 5 percent of mothers who have something bad happen, I focused on the 95 percent that don't.) I had a mantra too—"deflect, deflect, deflect"—whenever I came across fear-inducing comments or reading material.

KATHRYN: BECOME LESS REACTIVE

I had a breech baby, and I did all I could to deal with the condition that was bringing up my fears (like arranging for a midwife who had done a lot of breech deliveries). I also avoided people I knew would fuel my fear. For those people I couldn't cut out of my life, like my mom, I asked them *not* to mention any fear or worry about the breech. I would also steer the conversation away from the breech with people I knew would talk about their fear.

Most important, I learned not to react to people who feed fear. I learned to tap my inner resources of prayer and faith and simply disregard the fear-inducing comments. I also learned to be less reactive and more trusting whenever I was reading up on the subject of breech in various sources, some positive and encouraging and some quite negative. This was all good inner work, but not exactly fun!

SARAH: KEEP A JOURNAL

I kept a journal throughout the entire pregnancy. Writing helped me break my fears apart instead of having one big mass of fear.

DONNA: TURN OFF THE NEGATIVE AND TURN UP THE POSITIVE VOICES

I turned off those baby TV shows that only made me cry in fear (because all of the women were in so much pain), and I also listened—really listened—to what positive, reassuring people were saying to me. Every time I felt sad or scared, I could tell it was because my fear was louder than the reassurance I was getting from my friends and family, so I just made a choice to make their voices "louder" than my fear. It really helped.

KAREN: BREATHING EXERCISES

Whenever I had time, I'd do a simple breathing exercise. I'd sit and imagine breathing into the floor, then breathing into the space above me, and finally breathing into the center of my chest. Then I'd imagine breathing white light in and down my spine and up my spine. It's an exercise that reminds you to stay grounded.

Be Your Old Self Once Again

When we're pregnant, we often become absorbed in the pregnancy and forget that we once did anything other than think about it. Of course, there's nothing wrong with focusing a lot of attention on the new direction your life is taking. But once in a while it's also healthy to take a break and remember that there are other things in life. Instead of fretting, consider doing some of these activities:

1. Celebrate a birthday. Now is the time to honor your friends' birthdays. It allows you to focus on someone else's happy day, and besides, next year it won't be so easy to get away.
2. Visit a museum. It's fun to steal away and get lost in the artwork, but more important, art also demonstrates the transparency of time.
3. Grow something (other than what you're obviously already growing). I started a butterfly garden. I still enjoy the plants, and I like thinking about how I planted them when I was seven months pregnant. Herbs and flowers are also great because they're useful—you can make bouquets with both—and they can be planted in pots.
4. Listen to music. Skip that stuff that's supposed to enrich the baby. Just listen to music that you love and that makes you feel good.
5. Volunteer. I volunteered for an organization that helped homeless kids. Karma-wise, it makes sense; you help someone else's child, and perhaps if/when your child needs help, someone will be there in turn.
6. Read a nonpregnancy book. I'm always up for good literature or classics, but many women love mysteries, romances, or biographies. You could decide, for instance, that you want to read as many biographies of first ladies as possible in nine months.
7. Start something. I've known pregnant women who've started exploring totally new interests, such as landscape architecture. This may sound counterproductive; people will advise you not to start anything because you'll soon be consumed by the baby. Yes, you are going to be consumed by the baby, but there's nothing wrong with getting your feet wet exploring something you've long desired to study. You can slowly get back into it again once the baby is older.
8. Finish something. One of my friends had only a few units left to finish her bachelor's degree. When she found out she was pregnant, she was determined to get her degree before the baby came. And she did. She didn't walk across the stage at graduation, however; she was a tad busy giving birth.
9. Take a nonpregnancy exercise class. Although pregnancy workout classes and prenatal yoga offer great support and camaraderie, it's also nice just to get away and exercise with regular folks.

10. Pamper yourself. Manicures, pedicures, and massages are great, but don't put off regular maintenance like getting your teeth cleaned. This, in particular, is very important, because pregnancy hormones cause more gingivitis and also because you may not have a lot of time for appointments after the baby comes.

11

Fearless Postpartum (Epilogue)

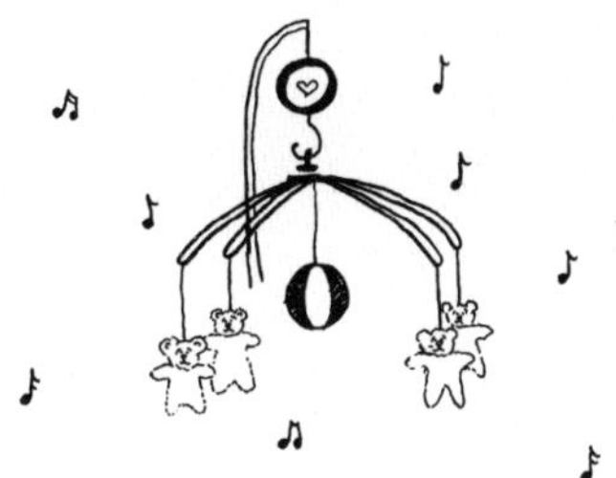

The postpartum period, one of the most important times in a woman's life, is usually the least discussed. Of course, everyone anticipates the baby's arrival, but few consider how the mother will feel emotionally and physically after the delivery.

Many cultures adhere to the forty-day rule. In Biblical times, women were honored for forty days after giving birth by being taken care of by other women. In some societies, women are still pampered and not expected to do much for forty days after delivery. In our fast-paced American society, more often than not women are expected to be out shopping at Wal-Mart forty minutes after they get home from the hospital!

There should be a happy medium. The postpartum period is a very precious time when a woman's physical and mental state can be fragile. If you've already had a baby, you know this. If this is your first, however, a little prep work can go a long way toward making that first month much easier.

Four Ways to Make Your Postpartum Period Easier

1. **Prepare what you can ahead of time.** The more shopping, meal preparation, bill paying, organizing, or laundry that you can do before the delivery, the better. Take care of as many odds and ends as possible in the weeks before your due date.
2. **Ask for help.** If someone wants to come see the baby and asks what they can bring, tell them *food.* The greatest gift someone can give you is a meal.
3. **Learn to let go.** Expect that your house will be messy, the dog's toenails will not get clipped, and you will probably run out of toilet paper. These are all lessons in child rearing. You will soon find your whole life takes on new meaning. Although you used to get ten things done in a day, with a newborn you will be lucky if you do one or two.

4. **Enjoy your baby.** If you're a real go-getter, you may find it hard to let things go and to just relax and stay home. Try to remember that your baby will be this small only once. Relish every little yawn and stretch, the sweet baby smell, and the first smile. Try to savor every moment, pamper yourself as much as possible, let your body heal, and allow yourself time to fall in love with your baby.

A Postpartum Tip: Be Flexible

The postpartum period has to be a time of flexibility. You can't know how you will feel, how fast you'll recover and regain your figure, or how to prepare for the life changes you've never before experienced. Be kind to yourself, be patient with your loved ones, and try to express your desires and needs openly.

Some of you will cruise through this time. Others will feel depressed, overly tired, and disappointed that they are not the bubbly new moms on sitcoms. The best solution is not to be alone at this time. Long before you deliver, try to arrange for your husband, a family member, or hired help to be with you at least for the first few weeks. Some practitioners will want you to come into the office after one or two weeks and again at six weeks so they can see how you're doing. We all answer our pagers twenty-four hours a day and are available for questions and conversation if that's what's needed. Remember, though, to direct baby questions to your pediatrician.

Your Body Postpartum

Here are some of the common things you can expect in the first six postpartum weeks:

BLEEDING

After delivery, you will bleed quite heavily for the first twenty-four hours. Then it will taper off to a flow similar to a heavy period. This will continue for a few days or up to a week. After that, you will experience some light bleeding for anywhere from two to eight weeks. If you're on your feet too much, you will bleed more heavily. If you notice your bleeding is increasing, it is a signal for you to slow down and rest more.

After about one week postpartum, if you suddenly pass a clot the size of an egg, don't panic. This does happen occasionally. If you pass more than one clot bigger than an egg and blood is running down your legs, though, that's too much. Get off your feet and call your health care practitioner. Also, postpartum bleeding, called lochia, has a distinct odor that is not foul smelling. Use pads, not tampons, and call your doctor or midwife if you notice a change to a more unpleasant odor.

CRAMPING

Menstrual-like cramps are common—especially if you're breast-feeding—for the first three to five days after delivery. This is nature's way of shrinking your uterus and limiting blood loss.

You should always use pads, not tampons, and avoid intercourse (in fact, the thought of sex may not even enter your mind). If the cramps are severe, you may need a narcotic-type pain pill. As soon as possible, though, switch to ibuprofen (if you are not allergic), since it works quite well on cramps. Narcotics are also very constipating, which is yet another reason to avoid them. None of these medications will affect your breast milk adversely if they're taken for short periods of time.

PERINEAL OR INCISION PAIN

After a vaginal delivery, your bottom will hurt whether you had an episiotomy, a laceration, or nothing. Some women feel vaguely uncomfortable, while others feel miserable. The best thing is keep ice on your bottom for at least twenty-four hours. Most of the discomfort is from swelling, and ice works wonders for this. Ice and a light painkiller such as Motrin may be all that's needed.

Since your urine is rather acidic, it may burn when you go to the bathroom. This will feel very much like putting lemon juice on a paper cut. Urinating while showering or using a squirt bottle of water when you pee are helpful hints.

It's also normal after giving birth to have some loss of bladder sensation and to occasionally leak urine. Over time, this will correct itself. Performing Kegel exercises will also help (see chapter 4).

Some women complain that they feel like their vaginas are going to fall out. That will not happen, of course, despite what you think. The discomfort is often a sign that it is time to rest more.

Your bowel habits shouldn't be affected, although you may develop hemorrhoids from pushing if you don't already have them. There are creams that are helpful, and these are usually standard fare in your postpartum orders.

CESAREAN-RELATED DISCOMFORT

For those women who deliver by cesarean section, the immediate postpartum period is bound to be different. Sometimes postpartum discomfort after a c-section can be more intense, so don't resist the prescription for pain relief that your doctor has written for you (although you may find it desirable to switch from a narcotic-type painkiller to Motrin or something like it a day or so afterward). Usually, you'll receive pain medicine in your epidural or spinal that will work very well for about eighteen hours. After that, take what you need in order to be mobile and enjoy your recovery. You can also ask for medicine for nausea and to help you sleep, and you also may be given a stool softener. All of these medications are safe for nursing mothers, so have no fear.

After the birth, you'll have a catheter overnight to drain your bladder, but this will be removed the next morning. Bladder and bowel habits usually return to normal quite rapidly after a cesarean section.

You can expect to go home on the third or fourth day after your delivery, but you'll be asked not to drive for two weeks and to avoid strenuous exercise for six. Your incision heals very quickly on the inside, and within two weeks your abdomen should have more than 90 percent of its strength back. Any increased pain, redness, oozing, or bleeding from the incision, though, may signify a problem. Call your doctor if you notice this.

When to Call Your Doctor

Call your health care practitioner if you experience any of the following postpartum symptoms:

- Heavy bleeding
- Extremely foul-smelling bleeding or discharge
- Severe pain anywhere that doesn't seem right and that won't go away
- Fever higher than 100.4 degrees
- Severe breast pain or expanding redness of the skin in this area
- Severe depression

On Exhaustion

FEARLESS Midwife

I often compare the aftermath of giving birth to being hit by a car. Most women feel achy all over, have back and leg pains, are swollen everywhere, and generally feel "beat up." I promise, though, that each day will get a little better, and by one week postpartum you'll truly feel like a new person.

That new person, though, will be extremely tired. Rest as much as possible! Once you have a baby, you are on a twenty-four-hour clock, and you need to behave accordingly. Sleep whenever you can, and forget about the idea of sleeping only at night. When you're more rested, you'll be able to cope better physically and mentally, and your whole life will take on a new light.

When Moods Swings Are More Serious

FEARLESS Midwife

After delivery, your body goes through many changes, and one of the most profound is hormonal changes. Most women feel moody, cry easily, and even fight more easily. This is all normal. Even throwing a book at someone can still be considered pretty routine postpartum behavior.

Some women, however, will sink into a deep depression or even a psychotic state. Your family members and you need to watch for signs of this, especially if you have a history of depression, etc. Call your health care provider immediately if you feel severely depressed, can't seem to find the energy to get out of bed or take care of your baby, or are having abnormal thoughts and feelings (such as fantasies of harm coming to yourself or your child). There are many great medications and counselors available to help. Feeling this way is not your fault, and it isn't something you'll live with for the rest of your life either. It's a postpartum symptom that will be resolved, but it does require treatment.

From the Fearless Midwife: Postpartum Anti-crash Plan

If you've never lived through a postpartum experience before, it's difficult to imagine what your life will be like for the first month after giving birth. Most women tend to think that you feed a baby, change the diaper, burp the baby, and expect your newborn to sleep without disturbing you for the next three or four hours. They envision working from home, making curtains, watching movies, and getting caught up on their reading while their little angels blissfully slumber down the hallway in their perfectly decorated little rooms. Some new mothers may even look forward to having time off from work and relish the thought of having "nothing to do all day." They can't imagine why people say they will need help after they have the baby.

Occasionally I do encounter a woman who doesn't need help and has all her little ducks in a row right away. Actually, I've encountered this maybe once or twice in my whole career! For the rest of us, life is very different postpartum. Here's how it usually goes.

Quite a fervor surrounds the arrival of the baby. There are gifts, visitors, flowers, and countless phone calls. Your partner takes time off work for a few days or a few weeks, and life is great. You adore your baby and couldn't be happier. Then reality sets in. You're alone day-in and day-out with the baby. You have all of the household chores and errands to do because your spouse assumes you should be able to handle them. After a couple of weeks of sleep deprivation, your nerves are frazzled. You get run down, catch a cold, fight a lot with your partner, cry easily, and soon are at your wit's end. Why does this happen?

The answer is really quite simple. Few women realize what they are getting into until they've walked in the shoes of a new mom or, we should say, slippers, because it's often difficult for many new moms just to get dressed! Even if your baby is a perfect angel, the postpartum period can be daunting.

I find that the people who struggle the most are those who don't have a good support system or much help afterward. To be sure you're not one of them, make a plan. You wouldn't attempt to climb Mount Everest without a plan, right? My advice for your postpartum weeks is to plan ahead and have a realistic idea of what you're embarking on. Here's what I recommend:

Adopt a royal attitude.

Your body will go through a tremendous recovery period, both physically and emotionally. Your two main needs will be rest and help. Be prepared to admit that you need the help. Ask for it, and get it one way or another. When people offer assistance, take them up on it. If they don't, plan to ask anyway.

If we were all made of money and could employ an entire domestic staff, I'd recommend hiring a housekeeper, chef, chauffeur, personal assistant, and laundress. For most of us, our family and friends will have to fill these roles as much as they're able and willing. Overall, just plan to be a princess! Even if it's not in your character, try hard to become one and to ask people to help you. You will recover better and faster, and everyone will be happier in the end.

Be realistic about your partner.

Your mate will be new at all of this stuff too and won't quite know what to make of it. He will regress at the same time that your expectations rise. If your husband is less than helpful before the baby, he will be even worse once the baby is here. Do not expect that by some miracle he will suddenly know how to cook, will volunteer to scrub the toilet, or will believe that washing a dish is something human beings do. If your gut instinct is that he won't be very helpful, accept this fact and find someone who will. Right after you have a baby is not the time to argue about how he is never any help around the house; you already know that.

If you want to change him, you need to start working on him during the pregnancy (or well before). These things take time. Otherwise, you're setting yourself up for disappointment that will only make life more difficult.

Surround yourself with helpful, lovely people.

If you don't know anyone you can ask for help, call a local church and it will send someone right over (okay, I'm kidding). Really, though, do plan to invite only those friends and family members you know will be good for you. The ones who aren't good for you don't get invited.

I'll never forget my sister making tea in a pot and bringing it to me on a tray with a flower and cloth napkin. I practically burst into tears because it was such a sweet gesture and made me feel so nurtured. These are the things that restore you and fill your heart with happiness.

Plan an open house or visitor day.

I couldn't handle the volume of people who wanted to stop by to see the baby, and I didn't want to feel that every day the house, the baby, and I needed to be presentable for guests. Usually, I just wanted to be left alone to sleep! Instead, I planned a Sunday afternoon and invited several friends at staggered times, ordered deli trays from the market, and made my husband and mother-in-law do all of the clean-up. Everyone was happy, and I didn't stress more than necessary.

Be realistic about what you can do.

During the first week postpartum, there are only five things to accomplish every day: rest, eat, drink plenty of fluids, feed your baby, and go to the bathroom. Once you're up and around, you still need to continue to be realistic about what you can accomplish.

Every day I would make a list of what I needed to do (such as groceries, bank, post office, etc.). Then I'd prioritize and pick the top three most important tasks. I did this because I quickly discovered that my baby had her own rule—the rule of threes. She could be taken out of her car seat three times. After that, she cried nonstop, and if I didn't stop running my errands, we'd both be miserable.

It gets better with time. Babies become better humored about chores, but you have to learn their limits and work accordingly. Keep in mind that your baby will not have the same limits as your sister's baby or the kid down the street. So don't compare; just work with it.

Breast-feeding Woes

Entire volumes have been written, stores built, and leagues established just to deal with the issue of breast-feeding. There's a good reason. For many women, breast-feeding is difficult (at least initially). You can read about breast-feeding, you can take classes, and you can even attend La Leche League meetings in advance. All of this may help; at least you'll learn about the various breast-feeding holds. Then again, it may not help.

Here is what I learned from my breast-feeding experience:

It's probably not you; it's the baby.

Babies must learn how to breast-feed just as they learn later how to lift their heads, roll over, and sit up. The learning curve for bottles is much, much easier (instantaneous, usually). Why? Manufacturers have made it easy on infants by developing nipples that are really long in comparison to what you have. Your baby may be an extremely fast learner (the bigger the baby, the easier, as a rule), or he or she may be a little slower.

Of course, in some ways it does have to do with you, but not in a way that you can help. The shape of your nipple may make it easier or more difficult for the baby. If your nipples are flat or inverted, a simple plastic device may help the baby latch on and nurse more easily. A lactation consultant (at the hospital or who comes to your home) or a local breast-feeding store can "diagnose" your nipples and sell you the proper item.

It's not about trying hard.

All mothers who want to breast-feed (and we do strongly encourage you to consider it) try extremely hard. In fact, many a mother has sent herself to the brink of insanity trying to make this happen. It's generally not about trying hard, though. It's about trying long. If you try long enough, eventually most babies do learn how to nurse.

You'll have to supplement with a bottle and formula, of course, if your baby isn't getting the hang of things; your pediatrician will tell you about this. In fact, even if you do have to supplement with formula, you don't necessarily have to give up on nursing. I hooked up with some breast-feeding advocates before I gave birth to my son, and I was duly warned to absolutely not supplement lest the baby be plagued with nipple confusion. I took what they said to heart, but as I've often seen in life, being a purist about anything frequently backfires.

After a week of refusing to give my son the bottle, I finally had to give in. My milk supply hadn't yet come in adequately, and he wasn't having instant success. As I've often repeated since, he had no nipple confusion; he had a preference. For at least the first few months of his life he was committed to his bottle. I ended up stimulating my milk supply by pumping every few hours, and then I simply put the breast milk in bottles. It was both frustrating and time consuming. Just when I was ready to throw in the towel (and throw the pump out the window), my son started to nurse like a pro. Eventually, I completely stopped pumping, and he nursed beautifully. Of course, all babies and situations are different, so don't take this as a prediction of what will happen for you. It merely illustrates that time is often the answer.

Your partner will not know how to help.

When my son was about three months and our breast-feeding struggles were behind us, I had him with me in the grocery store. A sheepish and tired-looking man kept smiling at him and then finally commented to me about how aware and happy he looked. Of course, when anyone recognizes something special in your child, you instantly become Chatty Cathy (at least I do). I soon found out that his wife and he had recently had a daughter, and his wife was at home struggling that very minute with major breast-feeding issues. This guy was at the grocery store looking for healthy produce and food to buy his wife in a vain attempt to try to help in some way.

If you're struggling, your partner will be in anguish just as you are. He'll likely feel completely helpless (at least, my husband said he felt that way). Because every situation is different, the only thing I could tell the guy at the grocery store was what I'll tell you: Get in touch with a lactation consultant pronto if things are not working out, and, if possible, hang in there.

Using Bottles When You're Trying for the Breast

If you're forced to use bottles even though you're trying to get your baby to breast-feed, look for nipples that are as short and wide as possible. Lactation consultants often recommend the Evenflo Elite. Short and wide most closely resemble you, even though long and skinny nipples are the norm for bottles.

Lactation Consultants

Many hospitals now have highly trained lactation consultants who specialize in breast-feeding issues. The lactation consultant may help you while you're in the hospital and may also offer phone consultations or office appointments after you get home. Take advantage of this service if it's offered and you need it.

Another idea is to ask your OB/GYN, your local breast-feeding store, or your local chapter of the La Leche League for the name and number of a private lactation consultant. If you're struggling, lactation consultants are your best bet for breast-feeding success. You will most likely have to pay out of your pocket, and it won't be cheap (figure $150 to $300 for a house call), but you can submit it to your insurance company and are likely to be partially reimbursed.

Nursing and Dieting Don't Mix

FEARLESS DOC

Nursing requires you to drink lots of fluids and eat about 15 percent more calories per day than you need when pregnant. You will naturally lose some weight in these first six weeks. Some of you may get all the way back to where you want to be. Most of you will not, however, but don't try to diet while you're nursing. The first thing to go will be your milk supply. Rest assured that, over time and with exercise, the extra weight will come off.

The Breast-feeding Exaggeration

When my son was not more than ten days old, my husband and I took him and our dog to the park at the end of our street. It was a major outing, and I had the baby nestled securely in the sling. A couple walked by with their son in a stroller and, of course, had to peek in the sling (newborns will draw you like magnets too, after you have one). The mother got teary, which was sweet. Their child was seven months old, and to me he looked like a giant. When I noted how big he was, the father practically beat his chest and said, "Yep, 100 percent breast-fed!"

At the time, I was experiencing enormous problems trying to breast-feed, and if I hadn't been recovering from a c-section, I just might have kicked him (or not). What saved me from doing that or breaking down in tears was the look that came across the mother's face. It was the arched brow, hinting of more than a little bit of embarrassment. And then I recalled what I'd heard a friend say: Everyone seems to lie about how exclusively they breast-feed. I also remembered attending a few La Leche League meetings prior to my son's birth and noting that, curiously, a few moms there had bottles stashed in the bottom of the stroller or in a diaper bag.

In many parts of the country, breast-feeding is not such a big deal, but if it is where you live and you're having problems, please try to remember that almost everyone bottle feeds at some point, either because they must or because they choose to. There is also something you can do to ease breast-feeding tyranny. When you encounter new parents and the subject comes up, be honest about what you do. The fact that you breast-feed shouldn't be worn like a badge of honor. It's a way to feed your child, not something to brag about.

Say Oooooohhhh

When you're breast-feeding, make sure you don't tense your body. This happens especially when you're trying to get the baby to latch on and are having a bit of a struggle. Some people say tensing up impedes the whole process, but one thing is certain. It does nothing for your neck, back, and hands.

An easy way to ensure you're relaxed is to take note of your mouth. Are your lips tense and pursed? If so, consciously release the tension there. Think of the Campbell Soup Twins. You want your mouth to be like their mouths—a little "O."

To Get Help...

For information on correct breast-feeding positions and latch-on tips, log on to:

- www.lalecheleague.org.

Our Final Thoughts...

Remember the study we mentioned in chapter 1? Neuroscientists theorize that mothers are calmer, smarter, and braver due to, they believe, the way maternal hormones influence the brain.

If you're having a hard time during the first few postpartum months, try to keep in mind that these are actually brain training months. By the time your child is a year old, you'll be smarter, calmer, and, yes, so much braver. We're confident of that.

Index

A

Accutane, 129
acupressure wrist bands, 37
acupuncture, 226
AFP/triple marker screening, 49, 72
age, testing and, 53–54, 60
air travel, 146–147, 148
alcoholic beverages, 79–80
Alice, Kathryn, 225
alternate nostril breathing, 225
amniocentesis
 age and, 53–54
 compared to CVS, 62
 as definitive test, 56
 explained, 50, 73
 before induction of labor, 184
 miscarriage risk and, 61
 sexual relations after, 124
amnioinfusion, 200
anemia, 66, 67, 70
anesthesia, during pregnancy, 145
 see also pain management
ankles, swollen, 92
announcing of pregnancy, 31–33, 43–44
antibody screening, 65–66, 70–71
assertiveness, 40

B

back, avoiding strain on, 97
bathing, of baby, 159
batteries, 162
beauty routine, 128–133
 hair care, 128
 hand and foot care, 130, 133
 skin care, 132
 at spas, 131–132
 sun exposure, 129
 tooth care, 129
 see also body image
bed rest, 150–151
biophysical profile, 51
birth, *see* delivery
birth control, 126–127
birth plan, 185–189
bleeding
 early in pregnancy, 25, 43
 in placenta previa/placental abruption, 218
 postpartum, 234–235, 236
 sexual relations and, 124
blood banking, 197

blood pressure, routine testing of, 52
blood tests, 29, 65–68, 70–71
body image
husband and, 87–88
postpartum, 95
stretch marks, 91–92
swollen ankles, 92
varicose veins, 93–94
see also beauty routine; weight gain
body temperature, 131
bottle feeding, 164, 241–242, 243, 244
Bradley method, 180
bras, 115
Braxton Hicks contractions, 142, 143
breast pumps, 160
breast-feeding, 241–245
baby's reaction to, 241–242
dieting and, 244
husband and, 242–243
lactation consultant for, 241, 243
neck exercises and, 100
during subsequent pregnancy, 127
tension and, 245
weight and, 83
breathing
with alternate nostrils, 225
meditation and, 223–224, 228

C

caffeine, 79
calcium, 85
California Proposition 65, 139
car seats, 165–169
"carrier," of genetic disorder, 57, 58
cats, 139
cell banking, 197
cerclage, 216
Certified Nurse Midwife (CNM), *see* midwives
cervix, incompetent, 215–216
cesarean section, 204–209
postpartum period and, 206–207, 236
VBAC, 205, 209
childbirth education classes, 16, 180–183
childcare, at gyms, 99
chorionic villus sampling (CVS)
compared to amniocentesis, 62
as definitive test, 56
explained, 48, 72
miscarriage risk and, 61
sexual relations after, 124
chromosomes, 56. *See also* genetics
cigarette smoking, 122
classes, *see* childbirth education classes
Clayton, Victoria, 18
cleaning products and services, 140
clothing, 109–118
affording of, 111–113
fashion and, 116–117
sharing of, 111
for special events, 113
underwear, 115
colds and coughs, 134–136
complete blood count (CBC), 66, 70
confidence, in health-care providers, 17–18
contractions
Braxton Hicks, 142, 143
contraction stress test, 51–52
measuring during labor, 200
sexual relations and, 124
see also cramping
co-sleeper, 171
costs, *see* gear; health insurance
coughs and colds, 134–136
cramping
early in pregnancy, 25, 43
postpartum, 235
see also contractions

cravings, 81–82
cribs, 170, 172
CVS, *see* chorionic villus sampling
cystic fibrosis, 48, 57

D

dating of pregnancy, 27–28
delivery, 179–210
  birth plan and, 185–189
  cesarean section delivery, 204–209
  childbirth education classes, 16, 180–183
  common problems and treatments, 213–218
  doula and, 190–191
  husbands and, 189–190
  instruments and procedures for safe delivery, 198–203
  labor induction, 184, 185
  labor recognition, 192–193
  pain management, 194–196, 203
  vaginal delivery, 193
dental care, 129
depression
  postpartum, 236, 237
  during pregnancy, 137
diabetes, 63–64
  gestational diabetes, 63–64, 213–214
  testing for, 69–70
diaper smells, 164
diet, 29, 33–34, 43
  beverages in, 79–80
  good nutrition and, 84–85, 89–90
  morning sickness and, 37–38
  see also dieting; weight gain
dieting
  breast-feeding and, 244
  pregnancy and, 85–86
  see also weight loss
dilutional anemia, 67
doctors, *see* health-care providers; OB/GYNs
doulas, 190–191
Down syndrome
  screening for, 48–50, 56
  statistical risk of, 53
dreams, 227
drug testing, 70
due date, calculating of, 27–28

E

eating disorders, 90
eBay, 112
environmental hazards, 138–141
epidural, 195
episiotomy, 202–203, 235
equipment, see gear
exercise, 96–106
  neck and, 100
  postpartum, 98
  to relieve stress, 222
  scaling down of, 96, 103–105
  weightlifting, 103
  yoga, 101–102
exhaustion, postpartum, 237
expenses, *see* gear; health insurance
external fetal monitoring, 198–199

F

fake anemia, 67
false positives/negatives, 55–56
fashion, *see* clothing
fatigue, postpartum, 237
fear, 13–20
  commonsense and, 19–20
  origins of prenatal, 14–16
  physiology of, 19
fetal fibronectin, 217
fetal monitoring, *see* heartbeat (fetal)
Fischbein, Dr. Stuart, 18
fitness, *see* exercise

flat head syndrome, 163–164
folic acid, 90
foot reflexology, 130
footwear, 117
forceps, 200–201
fragile X syndrome, 57
fragrances and scents
  diapers and, 164
  nausea and, 131, 133
fruits, 85

G

gardening, 139
gasoline, pumping of, 138–139
GBS (Group B strep), 71
gear, 43, 155–176
  assembly of, 162
  basics of essential, 155–161
  car seats, 165–169
  play pens, 175
  registering of, 173
  sleeping and, 170–172
  slings, 174
  unneeded, 162–164
genetic ultrasound, 50–51, 73
genetics, 56–59
  genetic counseling, 59
  pregnancy weight gain and, 78
  screening for disorders of, 57
  stretch marks and, 91
gestational diabetes, 63–64, 213–214
ginger, morning sickness and, 37
gingivitis, 129
grooming, *see* beauty routine
Group B strep (GBS), 71
growth restriction, 214

H

hair color, 128
health insurance, 42–43, 44, 59
health-care providers
  birth plan and, 186–189
  first trimester visits to, 28–30
  when to call, 236
  see also midwives; OB/GYNs
heart rate (maternal), exercise and, 97
heartbeat (fetal)
  monitoring during labor, 16, 198–200
  nonstress test and, 51
  pregnancy confirmation and, 23, 29
hemophilia, 57
hemorrhoids, 94, 236
hepatitis B and C, 68
herbal remedies, 137
herbal teas, 80
HIV, 68
home pregnancy tests, 26, 28, 43
hormones, moods and, 40, 237
husbands
  breast-feeding and, 242–243
  childbirth education classes and, 181
  delivery preparation and, 189–190
  postpartum expectations and, 239
  pre-delivery travel and, 148–149
  weight gain and, 87–88
hydration, exercise and, 97
hyperthyroidism, 68
hypnobirthing, 203
hypothyroidism, 68

I

illicit drugs, testing for, 70
illnesses, 134–137, 147
incompetent cervix, 215–216
induction of labor, 184, 185
"informed consent" form, 16
insulin, 63
insurance, *see* health insurance
internal fetal monitoring, 199–200

"intrauterine growth restricted" (IUGR), 214
intrauterine pressure catheter (IUPC), 199–200
iron, 85

J
Jacobs, Lori, 166
jeans (maternity), 112
journaling, 222, 228

K
Kegel exercises, 98, 235
kick boxing, 104

L
La Leche League, 245
labor, *see* delivery
lactation consultants, 241, 243
Lamaze method, 180
lemons, morning sickness and, 37
libido, *see* sexual relations

M
macrosomia, 214–215
manicures, 130, 133
mantras, 227
massages, 131
mattress, for crib, 170
meconium, 200
medicines
 over-the-counter, 134–136
 prescription, 136–137
meditation, to relieve stress, 223–224. *See also* visualization
mental ability, enhanced, 14, 245
midwives, 17–18. *See also* health-care providers
miscarriage, 23–25, 43
 testing and risk of, 48, 61
mood swings
 postpartum, 237
 during pregnancy, 40, 43
morning sickness, 35–38, 43
 folic acid and, 90
 home remedies for, 37–38
 see also symptoms of pregnancy
mothers, 41, 58
multiple gestation, 215
muscular dystrophy, 57

N
National Highway Traffic Safety Administration car seat ratings, 165–166
"natural" delivery, 194–195
nausea, *see* morning sickness
neck, exercising of, 100
neural plasticity, 14, 245
neural tube defects, 49
noise, 141
nonstress test/biophysical profile, 51
nutrition, *see* dieting; diets

O
OB/GYNs, 17–18. *See also* health-care providers
"open house," 240
over-fifty-five fathers, 60
over-the-counter medications, 134–136
over-thirty-five mothers, 53–54
oxytocin, *see* Pitocin

P
pain management, 194–196, 203
 childbirth education classes and, 181
 postpartum, 235–236
paint fumes, 141
painting, to relieve stress, 222
Pap test, 29, 68
parenting classes, 182
parenting issues, 41, 44

pediatricians, 183–184
pedicures, 130, 133
perinatologists, 48
perineum, massaging of, 99, 179
pets, 144
Pitocin
to deliver placenta, 193
for induction of labor, 184, 185
in stress test, 51–52
placenta, delivering of, 193
placenta previa, 217–218
placental abruption, 218
plastic containers, 138
play pens, 175
polycarbonates, 138
postpartum period, 233–245
body changes during, 234–237
planning for, 233–234, 238–240
see also breast-feeding
prayer, 226
preeclampsia, 216
premature labor, 216–217
prenatal testing, *see* tests/testing
prescription medications, 136–137
prostaglandin, 184
proteins, 85
psittacosis, 144

Q

quadruple marker prenatal screen, 49–50, 72–73

R

reactions of others
to cesarean section, 207
to news of pregnancy, 31–33, 43–44
Rh factor, 65–66, 70–71
Rhogam, 65–66
risks, of everyday life, 121–122
see also specific issues
rubella immunity, 66–67

S

scents and fragrances
diapers and, 164
nausea and, 131, 133
sexual relations, 39
postpartum, 125–127, 235
during pregnancy, 39, 123–124
sexually transmitted diseases (STDs), 68, 69, 124
shoes, 117
sickle cell anemia, 48, 57
sit-ups, 102
skin problems, 132
sleep
of baby, 170–172
of mother, 150–151
slings, 174
"small for gestational age" (SGA), 214
smoking, 122
sonograms, *see* ultrasounds
spas, 131–132
spina bifida, 49, 50
spotting, *see* bleeding
STDs, 68, 69, 124
stem cell banking, 197
sterilization, of bottles, 164
stress
effects on baby, 142–144
ways to relieve, 221–230
stress test, 51–52
stretch marks, 91–92
strollers, 160–161
Stryker, Rod, 223–224
sun exposure, 129
surgery, during pregnancy, 145
swimwear, 115
sympathy weight, 88
symptoms of pregnancy, 26
syphilis, 68

T

talking, to relieve stress
 to oneself, 227
 to others, 221
Tay-Sachs disease, 48, 57
tests/testing, 47–73
 accuracy of, 55–56
 age and, 53–54, 60
 to confirm pregnancy, 23, 26, 28, 29
 to detect fetal abnormalities, 48–62, 72–73
 at first doctor's visit, 28–29, 64–69
 genetics and, 57–59, 72–73
 listed by trimester, 47
 miscarriage risk and, 48, 61
 of mother's health, 64–71
 prenatal screening, 29–30, 48–49, 56
 routine doctor's visits, 30, 52
 see also specific tests
therapy, to relieve stress, 221
thyroid testing, 68
tooth care, 129
toxoplasmosis, 144
transition, 193
travel, 146–149
treadmill running, 105
Trisomy 21 and 18, 48–49
twins, 215

U

ultrasounds
 baby's growth and, 214
 biophysical profile and, 51
 explained, 24
 genetic ultrasound, 50–51, 73
pregnancy confirmation and, 23, 29
umbilical cord, 186, 197
underwear, 115
urinary tract infections, 69
urination, postpartum, 235
urine, routine testing of, 29, 30, 52
uterine surgery, previous, 61

V

vacuums, used in delivery, 200–201
vagina, stretching of, 202–203
vaginal birth after cesarean (VBAC), 205, 209
vaginal delivery, 193
vaginal exam, 68–69, 71
varicose veins, 93–94
VBAC (vaginal birth after cesarean), 205, 209
vegetables, 85
"visitor day," 240
visualization, 225–226. *See also* meditation
vitamins
 morning sickness and, 37, 38
 nutrition and, 89–90

W

walkers, 159–160
water, 84–85
Weckl, Joyce, 18
weight
 pre-pregnancy, 28
 routine testing of, 52
weight gain, 77–95
 genetics and, 78
 husbands and, 87–88
 sensible diet and, 81–86
weight loss, after birth, 89, 94–95
weightlifting, 103
Wilson, R. Reid, 222, 225
"worry appointment," 222, 225
wrist bands, for morning sickness, 37

Y

yoga, 101–102, 105, 226

Resources

HEALTH

American College of Obstetricians and Gynecologists
Phone: 800-762-2264
www.acog.org

MIDWIVES, DOULAS, AND CHILDBIRTH EDUCATION

American College of Nurse-Midwives
Phone: 240-485-1800
www.acnm.org
www.midwife.org
(direct to midwife locator)

Midwives Alliance of North America
Phone: 417-923-MANA (6262)
www.mana.org

International Childbirth Educators Association (ICEA)
Phone: 952-854-8660
www.icea.org

Lamaze
Phone: 800-368-4404
www.lamaze.org

Bradley Method
Phone: 800-4-A-BIRTH
www.bradleybirth.com

BREAST-FEEDING

La Leche League International
Phone: 800-LA LECHE
www.lalecheleague.org

CESAREAN AND VBAC

International Cesarean Awareness Network (ICAN)
www.childbirth.org

ALTERNATIVE BIRTHPLACE OPTIONS

Waterbirth International
Phone: 503-673-0026
www.waterbirth.org

National Association of Childbearing Centers
Phone: 215-234-8068
www.birthcenters.org

About the Authors

Victoria Clayton is the Growing Up Healthy columnist for MSNBC.com and a well-known health freelance writer who has contributed to *Fit Pregnancy*, the *L.A. Times* magazine, *Redbook, Woman's Day, Health, Fitness* and many other publications. She had her first baby in August 2003.

Joyce Weckl, C.N.M., M.S.N., is a midwife at The Woman's Place for Health and Midwifery Care in Camarillo, California. She received a B.S. degree in nursing from St. Louis University in 1984. In 1993, she attended the University of Southern California and became a certified nurse-midwife. In 1995 she received a master's degree also from U.S.C. Her experience includes everything from high-risk obstetrics to home births. She has also worked in several birthing centers and hospitals and has served as an assistant clinical professor at the University of California at Irvine.

Stuart Fischbein, M.D., F.A.C.O.G., is an OB/GYN and fertility specialist in private practice in Los Angeles. He practices out of Cedars Sinai Medical Center. Dr. Fischbein also heads the Woman's Place for Health and Midwifery Care in Camarillo, CA. He's a member of the BabyCenter.com advisory board.